SUPREME COURT JUSTICES
SONIA SOTOMAYOR

SUPREME COURT JUSTICES
SONIA SOTOMAYOR

Sandra H. Shichtman

MORGAN REYNOLDS
PUBLISHING

Greensboro, North Carolina

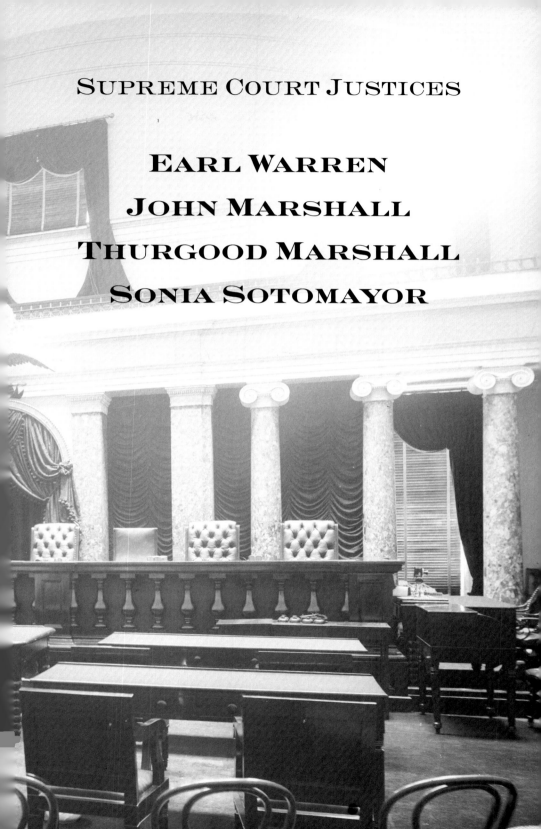

SUPREME COURT JUSTICES

EARL WARREN
JOHN MARSHALL
THURGOOD MARSHALL
SONIA SOTOMAYOR

Supreme Court Justices: Sonia Sotomayor

Library of Congress Cataloging-in-Publication Data

Shichtman, Sandra H.
 Supreme Court justices : Sonia Sotomayor / by Sandra H. Shichtman.
    p. cm.
 Includes bibliographical references and index.
 ISBN 978-1-59935-156-8
 1. Sotomayor, Sonia, 1954---Juvenile literature. 2. United States.
Supreme Court--Biography--Juvenile literature. 3. Hispanic American
judges--Juvenile literature. I. Title.
 KF8745.S67S35 2011
 347.73'2634--dc22
 [B]
                              2010020737

Printed in the United States of America
First Edition

To Ellen Rosenbush Smith, my dear friend and confidant

CONTENTS

Judge Sonia Sotomayor, the first Hispanic justice on the U.S. Supreme Court, is sworn in with the Judicial Oath in the east conference room of the Supreme Court on August 8, 2009.

THE LONG JOURNEY FROM A
PUBLIC HOUSING PROJECT

August 8, 2009 was a cloudy, warm day in Washington, D.C. A few minutes before noon, a door in the east conference room of the United States Supreme Court building on Capitol Hill opened. Sonia Sotomayor walked through it, followed by Chief Justice John Roberts Jr. in his black judicial robe. They came to a stop to stand at the front of the room, under the portrait of John Marshall, chief justice of the Supreme Court during the early years of the nineteenth century. In the audience was a group of about sixty people—mostly Sotomayor's family and invited friends—who had come to see Sotomayor sworn in as the 111th justice of the U.S. Supreme Court.

Sotomayor and Roberts were joined on the stage by Celina Sotomayor, the new justice's mother, and her brother, Juan, a physician from Syracuse, New York. Celina Sotomayor held the Bible on which her daughter placed her left hand. Sonia Sotomayor raised her right hand. In a firm voice she repeated the words of the oath spoken by Justice Roberts. "I, Sonia Sotomayor," she began, and repeated the remainder of the pledge that committed her to administer justice impartially, without regard to whether the people who came before the Supreme Court were rich or poor. When she had finished taking the oath, Justice Roberts shook her hand. "Congratulations and welcome to the court," he told her.

Justice Sotomayor gave her mother a long hug, then turned and hugged her brother. She was now at the pinnacle of her chosen profession. She was one of the most important people in the United States. Her decisions will help to determine the course of the country for decades to come.

Sonia Sotomayor had come a long, long way in her career. Unlike many who have made it to the highest court in the land she did not start from a place of privilege and has had to work doubly hard to prove herself as both a woman and as a Latina.

Sotomayor's parents were both born in Puerto Rico, an island in the Caribbean Sea located east of the Dominican Republic and west of the Virgin Islands that has been under U.S. control since the end of the Spanish-American War.

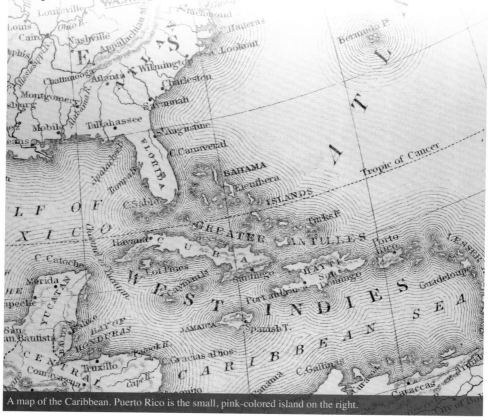

A map of the Caribbean. Puerto Rico is the small, pink-colored island on the right.

Sonia's mother, Celina Baez, was born in 1927 in Lajas, Puerto Rico. Her family was very poor. Celina's mother died when Celina was nine years old. Her father soon abandoned the family. When she was seventeen, Celina joined the Women's Auxiliary Corps (WACs), a branch of the United States Army. The WACs was created during World War II to do the jobs male soldiers left behind when they went off to fight in Europe and the Far East. Celina Baez was one of more than 150,000 women who joined the WACs. She was sent to the state of Georgia for training as a telephone operator.

Many years later, Sonia Sotomayor remarked about that time in her mother's life. "I can only imagine the culture shock my mom must have felt as a youth, somewhere between childhood and womanhood, trying to work in the South with a Spanish-only grammar school education," she said.

Celina Baez moved to New York City after she finished her service in the WACs, one of more than 30,000 Puerto Ricans who came to the United States during and just after World War II. They came looking for jobs and a better life than they had at home. Many of the immigrants went to New York City. Celina Baez settled in the Bronx; one of the five boroughs that make up New York.

Celina Baez got a job as a telephone operator in Prospect Hospital in the Bronx. She met and married Juan Sotomayor, who was born in San Juan, Puerto Rico. Juan left school after the third grade to go to work to help support his family. He could not join the United States Army because he had heart problems but, as did his wife, he emigrated from Puerto Rico to escape poverty. He found a place to live in the Bronx and went to work at a tool and die factory. The workers in the tool and die factory made specialized machine tools to be used in all types of manufacturing.

Sonia Maria was the couple's first child. She was born on June 25, 1954. A son, named Juan after his father, was born three years later.

During the 1950s and 1960s, New York City built many public housing projects that were intended to provide clean and modern apartments for poor and working-class families. Juan and Celina Sotomayor wanted a better life for themselves and for their children. Like thousands of other low-income families, they moved into a public housing project. They chose an apartment in the Bronxdale Houses in the Soundview neighborhood of the Bronx.

Sotomayor as a baby with her mother and father

The Bronxdale Houses, completed in 1955, consisted of twenty-eight red brick buildings. Each building was seven stories high. When the Sotomayors moved in, the apartments were clean and new. Their neighbors came from many different parts of the world, including many from Puerto Rico.

Parents could feel relatively safe letting their children go downstairs to play outside. But it was not perfectly safe. The people who moved into the apartments brought their problems with them. Many years later, Sonia spoke about the different kinds of people who lived in the Bronxdale Houses when her family did. "There were working poor in the projects," she said. "There were poor poor in the projects. There were sick poor in the projects. There were addicts and non-addicts and all sorts of people, every one of them with problems, and each group with a different response, different methods of survival, different reactions to the adversity they were facing. And you saw kids making choices." Some of the choices kids made were not good ones. They joined street gangs and got into trouble.

Sometimes life there wasn't easy, but Sonia remembered her years in the Bronxdale Houses fondly. She had many family members living nearby. "Being a Latina child was watching the adults playing dominoes on Saturday night and us kids playing loteria (a card game), bingo, with my grandmother calling out the numbers, which we marked on our cards with chickpeas," she said.

When she was eight years old, Sonia learned that she had diabetes. Her diabetes was called Type 1 diabetes, or juvenile diabetes, since it is the kind usually diagnosed in children and young adults. It is a disease in which a child's body doesn't make a hormone, or substance, that turns sugars, starches, and other foods into energy. Children with Type 1 diabetes usually feel very tired, thirsty, and hungry. They lose weight, even though they eat and drink healthy foods. They must take insulin in the form of injections in order for their bodies to work properly. Sonia was told she would have to take insulin shots every day for the rest of her life.

Sonia enjoyed reading, especially the Nancy Drew mysteries. Nancy Drew was a fictional amateur girl detective. The series was very popular during the 1950s, when Sonia was a young girl. Sonia decided she wanted to become a detective like Nancy Drew when she grew up, but was told that being a detective was too active a career for someone with diabetes. She began to think about the kind of career that she could have.

In 1963 Juan Sotomayor died of his heart problems. Now Celina Sotomayor had to support her children by herself. She knew that it was important for them to learn to speak English fluently. Spanish was the language they spoke at home, since Juan Sotomayor spoke only Spanish. Celina Sotomayor pushed her children to become fluent in English.

When she was ten years old, Sonia found the career she wanted to have. She was inspired once again by a fictional character. This time it was Perry Mason, a character she watched on television. "I became

Sonia Sotomayor grew up in the Bronxdale projects with aunts, uncles, and cousins living all around.

very disappointed about not having a life plan," she explained. "At the time, 'Perry Mason' had become a very popular show, and I loved Perry Mason. If I couldn't do detective work as a police officer, I could do it as a lawyer." She also saw that the most important person on the show was the judge. The judge decided whether the person on trial was innocent or guilty of the charges. But, in order to be a judge, she would first have to become a lawyer. So, at the age of ten, Sonia knew what her career goal was and what she needed to do in order to become a lawyer. "I was going to college and I was going to become an attorney (lawyer), and I knew that when I was 10. Ten. That's no jest," she said.

Celina Sotomayor knew that getting a good education was important for her children's future. She saved whatever extra money she could from her job and bought a set of encyclopedias for them to use for their school work. "I can remember the enormous financial burden that purchase placed on my mother," Sonia recalled when she was an adult. Celina Sotomayor also enrolled her children in Blessed Sacrament, a Catholic school in their neighborhood. She had to pay tuition for their education at Blessed Sacrament. "She struggled to put my brother and me through school," Sonia said many years later. "For my mother, education has always been the top priority in all our lives. It was because of her that we were the only kids I knew in the housing projects to have an Encyclopedia Britannica."

Sotomayor as a little girl

Years later, when Sonia Sotomayor appeared before a senate committee in Washington, D.C., she told the senators, "On her own, my mother raised my brother and me. She taught us that the key to success in America is a good education. And she set the example, studying alongside my brother and me at our kitchen table so that she could become a registered nurse."

Celina Sotomayor knew that a registered nurse earned good money. She also realized that her children would grow up and go off to live their own lives someday. "She knew that as a registered nurse she could survive without depending on us, and she wanted to give us the freedom to pursue our own lives," her daughter recalled. "It was no sacrifice at all for my brother and me to help my mom go to school."

Sonia explained her mom's drive to succeed. "My mom was like no student I knew. She got home from school or work and literally immersed herself in her studies, working until midnight or beyond, only to get up again before all of us," she said.

By the late 1960s, the neighborhood surrounding the Bronxdale Houses had changed. Crime had risen, gangs roamed the streets, and drug addicts sold heroin and other drugs in the halls of the buildings. The Sotomayors moved to Co-op City, a new housing development in the Bronx. "When we left, it was rough here (in the Bronxdale Houses)," Sonia's brother remembered years later. "Where we moved was clearly a step up."

Sonia was an excellent student at Blessed Sacrament. She graduated as valedictorian and went on to Cardinal Spellman High School, also a Catholic school. When her brother was ready for high school, he, too, went to Cardinal Spellman. By that time, Celina Sotomayor had become a registered nurse. She worked double shifts at the hospital's methadone clinic in order to pay for her children's education.

A childhood friend of Sonia's described Celina Sotomayor as a strict parent. She had rules that she expected her children to follow. "She worked, and basically no one was allowed out of the house until she came home from work," the friend remembered. But there was another side to Celina Sotomayor that Sonia's friends appreciated. "She would really listen, and she treated the teenager as someone with the chops (intelligence) to make a decision," recalled Sonia's friend from Cardinal Spellman High School, Kenneth Moy.

Sonia's apartment was a gathering place for her friends. They sat around the kitchen table discussing school subjects and world issues. Moy called it "a welcoming and communal place." The Vietnam War was one of the subjects that divided the group as it did many Americans. Some of Sonia's friends believed that the United States should not have become involved in the war. Others believed that it was the right thing to do. "Sonia was very much the ruler of the kitchen-table debate," Moy said. "She was very analytical, even back then. It was clear to people who knew her that if she wasn't going to be a lawyer, she was going to be in public life somehow."

Celina Sotomayor fed Sonia's friends as well as her own children. Sonia remembered the foods of her childhood. "My Latina identity also includes, because of my particularly adventurous taste buds, *morcilla—* pig intestines—*patitas de cerdo con garbanzo—*pigs' feet with beans—and *la lengua y orejas de cuchifrito—*pigs' tongue and ears," she told a reporter many years later.

Sotomayor in a cap and gown for her eighth grade graduation

Both the children's friends and members of the Sotomayors' extended family were welcome in the Sotomayor apartment. Kenneth Moy added, "When people in the family had troubles or concerns, they'd come to Celina and say, 'What do you think?'"

Sonia excelled at Cardinal Spellman just as she had at Blessed Sacrament. She was smart, worked hard, and was popular with her classmates. "When she would speak in class," said one of her classmates from Cardinal Spellman, "you always wanted to hear what she had to say about anything." "She was smart, she was disciplined. She was somebody who understood the idea that hard work had its own payoff," said another classmate. And a third classmate, who knew Sonia before they reached high school, said, "I remember at a very young age, her saying 'I want to make something of my life. I owe it to my family, to my mother and my brother.'"

Sonia was also a member of the National Honor Society. The Society was established in 1921. It recognizes outstanding high school students from across the United States for their academic excellence, leadership, service, and character.

There was one student at Cardinal Spellman High School who was special to Sonia. His name was Kevin Noonan. He and Sonia became high school sweethearts.

Sonia graduated from Cardinal Spellman in 1972. As she had been at Blessed Sacrament, she was class valedictorian. Kenneth Moy suggested that she apply for a college scholarship to attend Princeton University.

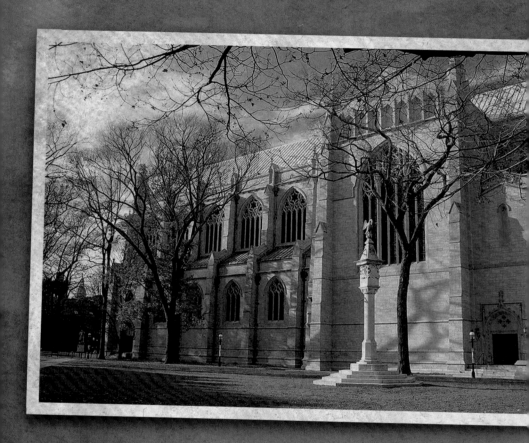

Princeton University Chapel

A SCHOLARSHIP TO
PRINCETON UNIVERSITY

Sonia Sotomayor took the advice her friend Kenneth Moy gave her. She applied for a scholarship to attend Princeton University in Princeton, New Jersey. She was accepted as a scholarship student in the fall of 1972.

Princeton is the fourth-oldest college in the United States. It was first chartered in 1746 and was called the College of New Jersey. Its first home was in Elizabeth, a city in New Jersey. A year later, the school was relocated to Newark, another New Jersey city. In 1896 its name was changed to Princeton University in honor of the city which became its permanent home. It offers classes in the humanities, social sciences, natural sciences, and engineering.

To be accepted as a student at Princeton was a high honor for a girl from the Bronx projects. Sotomayor would be attending school with students from an entirely different social class. Her friend Kenneth Moy, who was beginning his second year at Princeton, warned her what Princeton was like. "I told her I don't want you to come here with any illusions," he remembered. "Social isolation is going to be a part of your experience, and you have to have the strength of character to get through intact."

Sotomayor's Princeton yearbook picture in 1976

Sotomayor found that Moy's advice was accurate. "I felt isolated from all I had ever known," she later admitted. Many students had parents who were wealthy and could afford to pay the high price of a Princeton education. Many of them had graduated from prep schools, which are private high schools that prepare their students for college. They played tennis and went on ski trips in winter to places like Aspen, Colorado, and Davos, Switzerland. Very few of them had been raised in a public housing project in the Bronx.

Most of the students in Sotomayor's classes were male. There were very few women students and even fewer Latino students. For the first time in her life, Sotomayor realized that she was a member of a minority group. One of the professors who taught her during her freshman year remembered, "She was intimidated. She didn't speak in class." Sotomayor herself recalled her impression of the university during her first year there as "a very foreign experience for someone from the South Bronx" and said that she felt like "a visitor landing in an alien country."

Feeling uncomfortable about speaking out in class was only one problem. There were others. Sotomayor needed help with her writing and vocabulary skills. She admitted that her writing skills were inadequate. "I found out that my Latina background had created difficulties in my writing that I needed to overcome. For example, in Spanish we do not have adjectives. A noun is described with a preposition. My writing was stilted and overly complicated, my grammar and vocabulary skills weak."

She was unfamiliar with the classic books most of the other students had read when they were children. She recalled, "I spent one summer vacation reading children's classics that I had missed in my prior education—books like *Alice In Wonderland*, *Huckleberry Finn* and

Pride and Prejudice. My parents spoke Spanish; they didn't know about these books. I spent two other summers teaching myself anew to write." She had come this far and she was determined not to let these deficits in her education keep her from being successful in college. She got help with grammar and vocabulary from some of her professors and soon caught up with her classmates. She became confident enough to speak up in class as well. Her intelligence shone through and she began to excel in her classes. "She was very studious and intent on doing well in school," a friend said. "I remember her emerging sometimes in the early morning from her room, somewhat rumpled. I knew she spent all night working on a paper or studying. If she had a project to do, she worked on it 100 percent."

Sotomayor soon became involved in campus politics. She was aware of how few Latino students and faculty members there were at Princeton and wanted to help correct that imbalance.

There were many student organizations on campus at Princeton. One of these was called *Accion Puertorriquena* (Puerto Rico Action). Its purpose was to give Puerto Rican students more opportunities on campus. Sotomayor was invited to join and she did. Before long, she became its co-chair.

Sotomayor also joined other student organizations geared toward minority students. These groups gave her an "anchor I needed to ground myself in that new and different world" that was Princeton University. She became a member of the governing board of the Third World Center, a building on the Princeton campus where minority students could gather to talk, attend seminars and exhibits on subjects that concerned them, and take part in social and cultural events. Sotomayor became very vocal about the problems minorities, especially Latinos, faced at Princeton.

During her sophomore year at Princeton, Sotomayor complained to the university president, William G. Bowen, about the anti-Latino atmosphere at Princeton. The university responded in what Sotomayor considered a less than satisfactory way. Bowen defended the university and said, "We were committed to making progress, and we were making progress." But the progress the university claimed to be making was taking an unusually long time. Minority students weren't being admitted fast enough. Minority faculty and administration weren't being hired fast enough. So Sotomayor took the next step.

She and a group of Latino and Chicano (Mexican) students filed a formal complaint with the Health, Education, and Welfare Department (HEW) in Washington, D.C., on April 18, 1974. The complaint charged that there were no Latino or Chicano administrators or faculty members at Princeton. Only a token number of Latinos and Chicanos were admitted as students. And Princeton did not have a single permanent course devoted to Latino and Chicano cultures. Sotomayor's letter concluded, "The facts imply and reflect the total absence of regard, concern and respect for an entire people and their culture. In effect, they reflect an attempt—a successful attempt so far—to relegate an important cultural sector of the population to oblivion."

On May 10, 1974, she wrote a letter explaining the purpose of the complaint sent to HEW two weeks earlier. The letter was published in Princeton's campus newspaper, the *Daily Princetonian.*

Charles Hey was co-chair of *Accion Puertorriquena* along with Sotomayor. He explained the actions taken by the university as a result of the formal complaint. "The University began to make—I wouldn't say strides—but certainly a little bit of progress towards hiring faculty and recruiting, or being more open to the recruitment of students," he said. Within two years, Princeton had an affirmative action program in place. It showed how it planned to recruit more minority students and hire minority instructors, professors, and administrators.

In 1976 Sotomayor was one of two students to receive the M. Taylor Pyne Honor Prize. This was the highest honor that Princeton could give to an undergraduate student. "The prize, given to the senior or seniors who have 'manifested in outstanding fashion . . . excellent scholarship and effective support of the best interests of Princeton University,' carries with it an award equal to a year's tuition, $3,900 [in 1976]," The *Daily Princetonian* reported. According to that newspaper, the other student who received the honor was J. David Germany.

Twenty-five years later, Sotomayor spoke about the Pyne Honor Prize and what else she learned at Princeton. "The kid who didn't know how to write her first semester was honored for her academic excellence and commitment to university service with that award," she said. "In my years there, Princeton taught me that people of color could not only survive there, but that we could flourish and succeed."

Sotomayor also wrote a senior thesis. A thesis is a long research paper that colleges and universities require students to write before they can graduate. Students choose a subject and take a point of view and by using research gather evidence to support their point of view. Sotomayor chose to write about Luis Munoz Marin, the first democratically elected governor of Puerto Rico, and Puerto Rico's economic and political struggles during his time in office.

The thesis was titled *The Impact of the Life of Luis Munoz Marin on the Political and Economic History of Puerto Rico, 1930-1975*. In it Sotomayor concluded that, even though Munoz Marin brought much hope to his people for economic improvement, "the island has continued to be plagued by unemployment, absentee ownership and dependency on mainland revenues." Although more than forty years had passed since Puerto Rico became an independent territory of the United States, the island was still dependent on the United States for its economic survival.

Sonia Sotomayor graduated summa cum laude from Princeton University in 1976 with a bachelor's degree in history. Summa cum laude is a Latin phrase that means "with the greatest praise." It is used to show that a student graduated with the highest honors a school can award. "My days at Princeton . . . were the single most transforming experience I had," she said in a speech at Princeton years later. "It was here that I became truly aware of my Latina identity—something I had taken for granted during my childhood when I was surrounded by my family and their friends."

Peter Winn was a professor at Princeton. Sotomayor took his Contemporary Latin America course during her freshman, or first, year. Winn was also her advisor when she was writing her senior thesis. He later described the changes in Sotomayor during her four years in college. He said, "At Princeton, a tentative teenager—so intimidated that she never spoke in class during her first semester—became a poised young woman who negotiated successfully with top university administrators on contentious issues such as minority hiring practices. It was also there that Sonia Sotomayor more fully explored her ethnic identity."

She had come to Princeton from a sheltered life in the Bronx, New York. Princeton opened a whole new world to her and changed her forever.

The Sterling Memorial Library at Yale University

ON TO YALE LAW SCHOOL

onia Sotomayor needed to go to law school if she wanted to become a lawyer. She applied for and was awarded a scholarship to Yale Law School.

Meanwhile, she also focused on her personal life. In the summer of 1976 Sotomayor married her boyfriend, Kevin Edward Noonan. The couple had dated since they were students at Cardinal Spellman High School. The wedding took place in St. Patrick's Cathedral on Fifth Avenue in Manhattan. Sonia Sotomayor's name became Sonia Sotomayor de Noonan.

That fall she enrolled as a law school student at Yale University in New Haven, Connecticut. She had felt like an outsider when she arrived at Princeton, but it was quite different at Yale. Sotomayor felt comfortable at her new school. She felt as though she belonged there. A fellow law student said of her, "She seemed to fit in with everybody. Yale Law School typically has students that are very competitive, but she was loved by everyone."

She studied as hard at Yale as she had at Princeton. One of her professors at Yale remembered her as "very personable, intelligent, outgoing, extremely warm and very tough. She impressed me as an unusually brainy student even in this brainy group—and as someone who, by virtue of intelligence and drive, was destined for great things." A friend from Yale recalled, "She was always in the library, always had a casebook under her arm." But, although she was serious about her studies, "she always had a manner that was open. She didn't put down other people," he said.

She worked as a volunteer in the New Haven law office of David Rosen during one summer. "I remember her as quiet, capable, and very, very smart," Rosen said years afterward.

Sotomayor was as active in Yale's on-campus organizations as she had been in Princeton's. She continued to be an advocate for minority rights, especially for Latino rights. She wanted the university to hire more Latino faculty and to admit more Latino students. Her enthusiasm caught the attention of one of Yale's law professors, Jose Cabranes.

Jose Alberto Cabranes was also Yale University's general counsel, or head lawyer. He was born in 1940 in Mayaguez, Puerto Rico. He came to the United States with his family and settled in the South Bronx when he was five years old.

Sotomayor recalled meeting Cabranes for the first time when she accompanied a friend to a lunch meeting with him. Since they were both Puerto Rican and from the South Bronx, he and Sotomayor found much to talk about. Cabranes became Sotomayor's mentor and showed her how to work within the university system to advocate for the things she believed in. Their relationship would span more than thirty years. She later described him as a "career advisor," a "good friend," and an "intellect."

She became an editor of the *Yale Law Journal* and wrote an article that was published in its April 1979 issue. The article was called "Statehood and the Equal Footing Doctrine: The Case for Puerto Rican Seabed Rights." Sotomayor began by writing, "In the near future, negotiations between Puerto Rico and the United States will probably explore statehood as an alternative to the island's current 'commonwealth' status."

Since 1950 Puerto Rico has had commonwealth status, which meant that it had its own constitution and its own elected officials who took care of local issues, but is also a territory of the United States. By the

1970s people had begun talking about the possibility of making Puerto Rico the fifty-first state. There were opinions for and against it but, as one of Sotomayor's classmates recalled, it was "not a topic that was much in discussion at Yale Law School."

Sotomayor's article acknowledged that statehood was inevitable in the future. But she argued that the island should not give up the rights to the oil and minerals that lay under the ocean just off-shore when it becomes a state. Puerto Rico needs the money that drilling for those natural resources would bring. It would help improve the economy of the island, where many people still lived in poverty. She backed up her opinions with specific laws and court cases that agreed with her.

"Her work was thorough, dogged, careful and persuasive; steeped in legal sources and attentive to real-world consequences," another classmate said about Sotomayor's arguments in the article.

Sotomayor's interest in getting Yale to hire more Latino faculty and enrolling more Latino students continued. Since there weren't enough Latino students to form an organization specifically for them, she joined a group that represented students from a variety of minorities. She co-chaired the Latin American, Asian, and Native American Students Association. This group allowed its members to come together to discuss issues common to them all. Rudolph Aragon, who co-chaired the organization with Sotomayor remembered, "She was not a radical. I've seen people try to portray her as an ethnic radical. She was far from that."

Sotomayor took part in other campus activities and organizations as well. She was managing editor of the *Yale Studies in World Public Order*, a journal for Yale law students where they could write about issues of international law. Sotomayor took part in the Barrister's Union, a mock trial (simulated or pretend) competition among law students. The competition gives law students the chance to practice the skills they need in order to become trial lawyers.

By 1978 Sotomayor and her classmates began interviewing with law firms, hoping to be offered a position with one when they graduated the following year. In October Sotomayor attended a recruiting dinner. One of the partners in a large, well-known Washington, D.C., law firm, Shaw, Pittman, Potts & Trowbridge, spoke to her. One of the questions he asked her was "Do law firms do a disservice by hiring minority students who the firms know do not have the necessary credentials and will then fire [them] in three to four years?" The question implied that minority students were not as smart as other students. Another question implied that Sotomayor had been admitted to Yale Law School only because she was Puerto Rican. She felt that the questions were "discriminatory" and challenged that partner the following day at a formal interview. She told him that his questions the previous evening were insulting to her. He denied that he had meant to insult her. When he invited her to come to Washington for a second formal interview, she turned him down.

But Sotomayor didn't stop with refusing to have another interview. She filed a complaint of discrimination against Shaw, Pittman, Potts & Trowbridge. Yale had a student-faculty tribunal, which decided on such matters. Sotomayor's complaint triggered a campus-wide reaction. The tribunal ruled in favor of Sotomayor and demanded that the law firm issue an apology. Otherwise they could no longer recruit Yale graduates. The tribunal refused to accept the first letter of apology because "the firm did not seem to recognize the consequences of its partner's action." The firm's senior partner wrote the second letter. He admitted that the partner's questions were "insensitive and regrettable," and that "they may have had a chilling effect on the firm's recruitment of minorities and other students." Both the tribunal and Sotomayor accepted the second letter of apology.

Sonia Sotomayor was about to graduate from law school, but without the promise of a job.

Yale University

U.S. district attorney Robert Morgenthau

IN THE DISTRICT
ATTORNEY'S OFFICE

I n 1979 Sonia Sotomayor graduated from Yale Law School with a J. D. (Juris Doctor) degree. Juris is a Latin word that means law. A Juris Doctor degree is given to a person who completes his or her study of law. Sotomayor now had a law degree, but no job. That would soon change.

Manhattan district attorney Robert Morgenthau was recruiting at Yale Law School for graduates he could hire to work as assistant district attorneys in his office. Born into a political family in 1919, Robert Morris Morgenthau had been elected Manhattan's district attorney in 1975. A Yale Law graduate himself, he returned to the school each year to recruit new lawyers for his office.

During Morgenthau's visit in 1979 he ran into Jose Cabranes, Sotomayor's mentor. "I asked him if he knew anyone special I should speak with and he said, yes. He said the remarkable student named Sonia Sotomayor was deciding where to work. And while he did not know whether she'd given any thought to being a prosecutor, it would be well worth my while to meet her," Morgenthau said years later, when he spoke at Sotomayor's confirmation hearings designed to determine whether or not she should become a Supreme Court justice. "I told him to have her call me, and she did," Morgenthau said.

Sotomayor hadn't thought about working as a prosecutor, a lawyer who conducts proceedings against people accused of having committed crimes. But she liked the idea of helping to "to bring law and order to the streets of New York," so she accepted the job and moved back to New York in 1979.

"She was right out of law school. And what impressed me was her ability to move almost seamlessly from studying law from law books to being an assistant district attorney in a large urban environment—with legal issues and factual issues that are not the subject of any law school curriculum," recalled her supervisor, John W. Fried.

Besides working at her new job Sotomayer had to study and prepare to take the bar exam. It is not enough for lawyers to have a law degree. They must also pass a test, called the bar exam, that proves they know all about the laws in the state in which they want to work. Sotomayor took and passed the New York State bar exam in 1980.

In the early 1980s New York City experienced a very high crime rate and had severe drug problems. New Yorkers were afraid to walk on the streets or ride in the subway, especially at night. Robert Morgenthau and the district attorney's office worked hard to clean up the city. His office

The Court district in New York City

prosecuted criminals and drug dealers. It dealt with all kinds of crimes from misdemeanor thefts to murder.

The police arrested people they thought had committed crimes. The assistant district attorneys went to court when those people went on trial. It was the lawyers' job to prove that the person on trial had really committed the crime.

Part of Sotomayor's job was to appear in court. At first she was nervous. A more experienced prosecutor in the office who was training her said later, "I just remember at that particular point, she was like all the others that start: scared to death to go in front of a criminal court judge." But she soon overcame her nervousness.

"My work ran the gamut of criminal activity," Sotomayor remembered. "It was wonderful training for a lawyer." She prosecuted assault, or physical attack, robbery, child pornography, police brutality, and murder cases.

At first, Sotomayor was assigned to prosecuting minor crimes. She found herself feeling sorry for the people who committed them. They were generally poor and uneducated, like the people she had grown up with in the public housing projects of the South Bronx. "I had more problems during my first year in the office with the low-grade crimes— the shoplifting, the prostitution, the minor assault cases. In large measure, in those cases you were dealing with socioeconomic crimes, crimes that could be the product of the environment and of poverty," she explained.

But once she began prosecuting major crimes, or felonies, such as murder, rape, and arson (setting fires) she felt different. "Once I started doing felonies, it became less hard," she admitted. "No matter how liberal I am, I'm still outraged by crimes of violence. Regardless of whether I can sympathize with the causes that lead these individuals to do these crimes, the effects are outrageous."

She also continued to advocate on issues that concerned minorities, especially Latinos. She became a member of the Board of the Puerto Rican Legal Defense and Education Fund in 1980 at the urging of Jose Cabranes. It sought to assist Latinos against discrimination in the areas of education, housing, jobs, and voting rights. The head of the organization at the time recalled that Cabranes "was her patron, her mentor. He knew her. He thought she was a good fit." Sotomayor remained with the organization until 1992.

Tarzan of the Apes

of the

Apes

Edgar Rice Burroughs

In 1983 Sotomayor assisted a more experienced lawyer, Hugh Mo, in the prosecution of a high-profile murder case that became known as the "Tarzan" case. A man named Richard Maddicks was arrested and charged with breaking into almost two dozen apartments in Harlem, a neighborhood in the northern part of Manhattan. He entered the apartments by swinging down from the roof on a rope and stealing items from them. In connection with the burglaries, he shot several people and killed three of them.

Tarzan was a fictional character created by the author Edgar Rice Burroughs early in the twentieth century. Movies about Tarzan's adventures were popular beginning in the 1930s. In the stories Tarzan was raised by apes in the African jungle after his parents died. Like the apes, Tarzan could swing from tree to tree by clinging to the vines that hung from them. Because Richard Maddicks could swing down from the roof of a building, people called him "The Tarzan Murderer."

To prepare for the trial, Sotomayor visited crime scenes along with armed police officers. Sotomayor impressed both Mo and their boss, Robert Morgenthau. "She had that uncanny ability of putting together a complicated set of facts and distilling them into a very simple story that would resonate with the jury. That's unusual for a young attorney," Mo recalled. When the trial was over, Maddicks was convicted of the crimes. The judge sent him to prison for more than sixty years.

In 1982 the Supreme Court of the United States had confirmed that New York's laws against child pornography were constitutional. That meant that New York's district attorneys could prosecute people who were accused of taking photographs of naked children or children having sexual relations with other children or adults and selling those photographs.

The following year Sonia Sotomayor prosecuted New York's first anti-pornography case. When Robert Morgenthau testified at Sotomayor's confirmation hearings many years later, he wanted to explain how well she prosecuted that case. "Assistant DA Sotomayor left the jurors in tears over what the defendants had done to child victims," he told the senators of the Committee on the Judiciary, who were holding the hearings. One of the lawyers she went up against in another child pornography trial recalled that Sotomayor "handled it very well. She didn't pander to the jury. She was very methodical and well prepared."

Sotomayor learned a great deal about life during those years. "I saw children exploited and abused. I felt the suffering of victims' families torn apart by a loved one's needless death. And I learned the tough job law enforcement has protecting the public safety," she told the senators who were deciding on whether or not she should become a Supreme Court justice.

Besides her work as an assistant district attorney, Sotomayor started her own private law firm in 1983. She called it Sotomayor and Associates although she was its only member and her office was in her home. She explained that she helped "family and friends in their real estate, business and estate planning decisions."

In the district attorney's office, Sotomayor was thought of as a "potential superstar." But her married life was not going as well. By 1983 she and Kevin Noonan had been married for seven years. They had no children. Sotomayor spent hours doing research, finding and speaking to witnesses when she was not in court. Noonan had his own career. They had little time to spend together and had grown apart. They decided to divorce. "I cannot attribute that divorce to work, but certainly the fact that I was leaving my home at 7 and getting back at 10 o'clock was not of assistance in recognizing the problems developing in my marriage," she said years later when she looked back at that time of her life.

The Supreme Court Seal

A view looking down on Madison Avenue in New York City

ENTERING PRIVATE PRACTICE

Sonia Sotomayor spent five years working as an assistant district attorney. She successfully prosecuted criminals from pickpockets to murderers. But in March 1984 she left the Manhattan District Attorney's office and joined Pavia & Harcourt, a law firm with offices on Manhattan's Madison Avenue. "I left the criminal area because I wanted a broader experience personally in terms of lawyering," she explained. She joined the law firm as an associate, which is the entry-level position for a lawyer.

Her former boss, Robert Morgenthau, thought that there was a second reason why she left the district attorney's office after only five years. "It [her diabetes] made her think, 'I'm not going to be around forever, I have to keep moving.' I remember talking with her about how much time each day, about an hour, she spent giving herself shots of insulin."

Pavia & Harcourt was a commercial law firm. That means that its lawyers prosecuted businesses and business people who were accused of committing a crime. She was hired by George Pavia, the managing, or head, partner of the firm. "We had an opening for a litigator (trial lawyer), and her resume was perfect," he explained. "She was just ideal for us in terms of her background and training."

Sotomayor worked in the international commercial law area. "I focused on commercial, instead of criminal, matters," she said years later, when she spoke to the senators who were deciding if she would be a good candidate for the Supreme Court. "I litigated issues on behalf of national and international businesses and advised them on matters from contracts to trademarks." Her job included writing requests or pleas to the court at a client's request, getting information to be used during a trial, and going to court to prosecute a company or a person suspected of committing a crime against one of Pavia & Harcourt's clients.

One of the law firm's clients was Fendi, an Italian company that manufactured and sold expensive women's handbags. Fendi owned the trademark for the handbags, which meant that their handbags had a distinct look that no one was allowed to copy. But, even so, the luxury Fendi handbags were being copied and sold at low prices on the streets of New York and elsewhere. These low-priced copies are called "knockoffs" and it was illegal to manufacture and sell them. Fendi wanted to stop the knockoffs from being made and sold.

Members of the New York City Police Department raided warehouses where these knockoffs were stored and arrested the people involved. Sotomayor accompanied the police on several raids. "As a result, I had my own bulletproof vest and worked closely with law enforcement officials," she said. She had once wanted to be a detective, but was told it was too active a career for someone who had diabetes. "She had no fear," said one of her colleagues. "That's just her personality."

But the great majority of the work Sotomayor did was not as exciting. In 1986 she took part in a panel discussion on women in the workplace on TV's *Good Morning America*. She explained then that most of the time being a lawyer means doing drudgery work such as sitting in the library, writing briefs, and having long conversations with clients.

She also mentioned the toll working long hours took on a lawyer's personal life. By then she had been divorced from Kevin Noonan for three years. She had no time for going out socially with friends or for dating. She said that if a man asked her three times to go out with him and three times she told him that she had to work late or travel out of town for her job, he might think she wasn't interested in dating him and stop asking.

But Sotomayor did make time to continue the charitable work she had been doing for years for poor and minority people. She continued her work with the Puerto Rican Legal Defense and Education Fund. Like other lawyers who were interested in helping Latinos achieve equal rights in voting, housing, education, and jobs, she worked pro bono for the organization. That meant that she received no money for her work. Pro bono is a Latin expression that means "for the good" and refers to doing something for the good of the people.

In 1986 she closed Sotomayor and Associates, the law firm she'd started in 1983 to help her family and friends with their legal problems. Years later, she described it as an informal consulting firm. She said that all she did was give legal advice to family members and friends, read contracts for them, and prepared a divorce agreement. She never filed legal papers for them and she never appeared in court on their behalf. If they "required more substantial legal representation, I referred the matter

Mario Cuomo

to my firm, Pavia & Harcourt, or to others with appropriate expertise," she said when she was nominated to be a Supreme Court justice.

The following year two of her colleagues at Pavia & Harcourt mentioned Sotomayor's interest in public service to the appointments secretary to Governor Mario Cuomo of New York State. "She floored us," was how the appointments secretary put it. The appointments secretary was so impressed with Sotomayor's background and experience that she recommended Sotomayor for the board of the State of New York Mortgage Agency (SONYMA).

The governor appointed Sotomayor to the mortgage agency, which helped people who do not earn a lot of money get loans so they could buy a house. "She was the youngest board member but extremely involved in the details," William Eimicke, the man who headed the agency at that time, recalled. The agency's executive vice president remembered that "she was very prepared and thoughtful, and a voice of mediation. I found her to be direct, which I liked." It was another pro bono job for Sotomayor.

As a result of the agency's work, construction companies built apartment buildings and homes in neighborhoods where homes and stores had been abandoned, broken into, and burned down. These were neighborhoods where the majority of people who lived there were poor and minorities.

The minutes from one of the New York Mortgage Agency meeting shows Sotomayor's concern for poor and minority people: "Ms. Sotomayor voiced her continuing objection to the rehabilitation of projects in low-income areas without providing for a higher component of low-income families. She repeated her request for an analysis of the various economic groups in the neighborhood affected by the project." Sotomayor insisted that the new construction projects set aside an adequate number of apartments and homes for low-income people.

In 1988 New York City created the Campaign Finance Board, a city agency that is still in operation. It distributes public money for political campaigns in the city. Candidates for city offices can apply to have the city match the amount of money they raise from individual contributors. It publishes a voter's guide, which educates voters about the candidates running for various political offices in the city. It also arranges for candidates to debate each other, another way in which to educate voters.

Mayor Ed Koch needed to appoint members to the agency's board. Robert Morgenthau recommended that Sotomayor be one of those members. As the district attorney he was very influential in the city and he assured the mayor that Sotomayor was the right person to become a member of the board.

Peter Zimroth, the lawyer for the city, interviewed her. "I remember when I finished the interview thinking that we had found a gem, that this was a straight shooter, a very serious lawyer who seemed absolutely independent," Zimroth said later. And Mayor Koch remembered, "I had a search made of the best people, and she was it." Sotomayor was appointed to the New York City Campaign Finance Board. "While there," Morgenthau said years later, "she continued to earn a reputation for being tough, fair, non-political in an arena where those characteristics were sorely needed." She worked very hard at this job just as she did at Pavia & Harcourt and at the state mortgage agency.

She received compliments on her work at the board from others, including its former chairman, the Reverend Joseph O'Hare, who remembered, "She was very tenacious." And she did not allow her diabetes to slow her down. "We would be in a tense interview with a candidate and she would be shooting herself with insulin in the back of the hand," O'Hare said. And just as she did with the Puerto Rican Legal Defense and Education Fund and the State of New York Mortgage Agency, Sotomayor worked pro bono for the New York City Campaign Finance Board.

That same year Sonia Sotomayor was promoted and became a partner at Pavia & Harcourt.

Daniel Patrick Moynihan

BECOMING A FEDERAL JUDGE

Even after becoming a partner at Pavia & Harcourt, Sotomayor continued her pro bono work for the Puerto Rican Legal Defense and Education Fund, the New York City Campaign Finance Board, and SONYMA, the state mortgage agency. It was because of her work with the city and state agencies that she began to attract the attention of state politicians.

In 1990 a seat on the federal bench for the Southern District of New York became vacant. The Southern District of New York encompasses the boroughs of Manhattan and the Bronx in New York City as well as Westchester, Putnam, Rockland, Orange, Dutchess, and Sullivan counties further upstate in New York. The seat had been held by Judge John M. Walker Jr., who was promoted to a seat on the United States Court of Appeals.

It was the job of New York's senators to gather names of qualified people who could fill the vacant seat and submit the name of the person they felt was best qualified to the Senate Judiciary Committee in Washington, D.C. If the Senate Judiciary Committee approved the nominee, his or her name would be sent to President George H. W. Bush. The president would then officially nominate that person to the federal bench.

George H. W. Bush, the forty-first president of the United States

New York's senior senator, Daniel Patrick Moynihan, was unhappy because the judges on the federal bench were mostly white males. He wanted more female and minority candidates to fill empty seats as they became vacant.

Sotomayor was urged by David A. Botwinik, another partner at Pavia & Harcourt, to apply for the vacant seat on the federal bench. "I had always wanted to be a judge, but I assumed it would happen much later in my career," she admitted later. "I was still in my 30s at the time and I felt they would not even consider me. If it hadn't been for my partner's insistence and support, I never would have applied."

"I just decided her name should be in the hopper," Botwinik said, meaning that Sotomayor should be one of the people considered for the seat. He sent Sotomayor's name to his friend Judah Gribetz, who headed senator Moynihan's judiciary screening committee. That group was responsible for looking at all the applications and recommending the most qualified person to the Senator. Sotomayor was interviewed by the committee members.

As a judge, she would need to be independent, to interpret the law without regard to pressure from politicians. "Sonia had no political connections and did not come through the political process, but these were social friends of mine. I trusted them," Gribetz said about Botwinik and others he spoke with who thought highly of Sotomayor. He and the committee agreed that Sotomayor was an appropriate choice for the seat. Her name was then sent to Senator Moynihan.

Moynihan was impressed with Sotomayor's background and achievement. "His interest was in the pursuit of excellence and in the pursuit of diversity, which are not mutually exclusive," Gribetz remembered years later.

When the senator asked Gribetz "Where did you find her?" he said he replied, "She came out of nowhere," but later told him, "Here's a gal that came out of the South Bronx and went to Princeton and Yale, was in Bob Morgenthau's office and is at Pavia & Harcourt, a nice law firm."

After interviewing Sotomayor, Moynihan agreed with her selection and submitted her name to President George H. W. Bush. The president forwarded Sotomayor's name to the Senate Judiciary Committee, whose job it was to investigate the prospective judge and either approve or disapprove the nomination.

Sotomayor had to appear before the committee to answer questions that they put to her. She said later, "The hearing was wonderful. Because a Democratic senator [Moynihan] had proposed me and a Republican President [Bush] nominated me, my questions were pro forma."

Her nomination was approved unanimously. Not a single member of the Senate Judiciary Committee voted against her. She was confirmed as U.S. District Court Judge for the Southern District on August 11, 1992. She was now the youngest judge in the Southern District and also the first Latina federal judge in New York State.

Sotomayor resigned from the organizations she'd been involved with so there could be no conflict of interest between her work for them and her work as a judge. She left Pavia & Harcourt on September 30. Her new office was in the Federal District Courthouse in Lower Manhattan.

One of Judge Sotomayor's first cases was one that concerned a law in White Plains, New York, that forbade anyone from displaying a religious symbol in a public place. In this case a rabbi wanted to place a nine-foot-high menorah in one of the city's parks during the Jewish holiday of Chanukah. A menorah is a candelabra that Jewish people light during the eight-day holiday.

White Plains maintained that to display the menorah in a public place violated the Constitution of the United States, which does not allow the establishment of an official religion in this country. Anyone can practice whatever religion he or she chooses. The rabbi said that the law violated his right to practice his religion freely.

In 1993 Judge Sotomayor ruled that the White Plains law was unconstitutional. Allowing the menorah to be displayed did not mean that the city was establishing an official religion. She wrote that a law cannot "preclude a private speaker from erecting a fixed display of a religious symbol, free-standing or otherwise, in a City park on the basis of such a display's religious message . . . The Establishment [of an official religion] Clause does not provide a compelling justification for the Resolution's [the White Plains law's] content-based restrictions on expressive conduct."

The following year, Sotomayor was involved in another religious issue case. A group of inmates in a New York prison wanted to wear colored beads under their belts. The inmates claimed that they practiced a religion called Santeria. They said that the beads were part of their

Downtown Manhattan federal courthouse

Lyndon B. Johnson, the thirty-sixth president of the United States

religion and were meant to keep evil spirits away. Prison officials claimed that the beads were gang symbols. They said that prison policy was that "inmates will be permitted to wear only tradition-ally accepted reli-gious medals, cruci-fixes, or crosses."

Sotomayor ordered prison officials to allow the wearing of the beads, saying that "the beads are not, as defendants would have me recognize, an optional devotional item. Rather, they are the hallmark of plaintiffs' beliefs." Her ruling was based on the fact that the first amendment to the U.S. Constitution guarantees all Americans the right to practice their religion as they wish.

During the years she served as a U.S. District Court judge, Sotomayor heard hundreds of cases. Sometimes she ruled in favor of the plaintiffs, the people who brought the cases to the court because they thought they had been wronged. In other cases, she ruled in favor of the defendants, the people who claimed no wrong had been done. Sotomayor's rulings were always based on her strict interpretation, or understanding, of what the laws involved in the cases actually said.

In 1995 Judge Sotomayor ruled in two cases that brought her to the attention of the national media. When Vincent Foster, a White House lawyer, was found dead in a Washington, D.C., park, his death was ruled a suicide. A note was found in his briefcase, which police said was a suicide note. The *Wall Street Journal*, a newspaper with headquarters in New York, sued to have the government release the suicide note. Sotomayor ruled that under the Freedom of Information Act the note had to be made public.

The Freedom of Information Act was signed in 1966 by President Lyndon Johnson. It assured the people of the United States that they could find out everything that is happening in the government and gave them a way to get the information that they wanted.

In her ruling that the Foster note be made public, Sotomayor acknowledged that doing so would affect the Foster family. They would be hounded by reporters who would want to interview them. "I sympathize with them for the pain they will bear as a result of any renewed scrutiny," she wrote. "I am not convinced, however, that any such renewed interest will be so substantial as to outweigh the important public interest in viewing the Note." The public had the right to know what was in the note.

That same year Judge Sotomayor ended the Major League Baseball strike, which had been going on for nearly eight months. The owners of the baseball teams wanted a cap, or limit, placed on players' salaries. They claimed that a salary cap would help them save money. The players opposed a salary cap and went out on strike on August 12, 1994, refusing to play baseball. The baseball commissioner cancelled the rest of the baseball season. Because of the strike, there was no World Series in 1994, disappointing baseball fans across America.

On March 31, 1995, Judge Sotomayor ruled in favor of the players, denying a cap on their salaries. The 232-day-old strike was officially over and the players went back to work two days later.

The baseball strike was an issue that Sotomayor felt strongly about, since she had been a fan of the New York Yankees for many years. "You can't grow up in the South Bronx without knowing about baseball," she said, explaining her interest in baseball to a newspaper reporter while the hearing in the case was going on.

Now Sonia Sotomayor's name was known to every baseball fan in America. "Some say that Judge Sotomayor saved baseball," said President Barack Obama when he spoke about her to an audience a few years later. Without her ruling, no one could be certain how much longer the baseball strike would have gone on.

In 1996 she presided over a lawsuit brought by the family of a man who died of AIDS, which stands for Acquired Immune Deficiency Syndrome. They claimed that the movie, *Philadelphia*, which starred actor Tom Hanks as a lawyer who was fired by his law firm because he contracted the disease, was based on what actually happened in their family. They claimed that the people who made the movie stole their story.

During the trial, the movie was played in the courtroom. There is a dramatic scene in the movie in which Hanks' lawyer, played by Denzel Washington, gives an impassioned speech in front of the judge, jury, and spectators. Judge Sotomayor warned the lawyers arguing the case before her not to repeat the scene in the movie. "I don't expect melodrama here," she told them. "I don't want anybody aspiring to what they see on the screen." The case was settled without Sotomayor having to reach a decision.

Some of Judge Sotomayor's rulings were reversed, or changed, by a higher court, the Court of Appeals. When a plaintiff or a defendant is not happy with a ruling in the U.S. District Court, they can appeal the ruling to the next higher court, in this case, the Court of Appeals. The Court of Appeals can reverse the ruling of a lower court judge.

In 1997 Sotomayor ruled in a case brought by freelance writers against the *New York Times*. These writers did not work for the newspaper but contributed articles that the newspaper paid them for and published. The writers claimed that the newspaper violated the copyright law by transferring the articles from print to electronic form and putting them into its electronic database. In this way, readers could access the articles for free on the Internet. Sotomayor ruled that the newspaper did not violate the copyright law, but the Court of Appeals reversed her decision.

That same year President Bill Clinton nominated Sonia Sotomayor to become a judge in the Court of Appeals for the Second Circuit. This would be a promotion for Sotomayor, but her confirmation for the seat would not take place for another year.

Bill Clinton, the forty-second president of the United States

Sonia Sotomayor

APPOINTMENT TO THE COURT OF APPEALS

I n October 1996 J. Daniel Mahoney, a judge on the U.S. Court of Appeals for the Second Circuit, died. That left a seat on the court that needed to be filled. A search began for a judge who could fill the vacancy. As he had done before, Senator Daniel Patrick Moynihan nominated Sonia Sotomayor.

The Court of Appeals is made up of thirteen actual courts. One is in Washington, D.C., and the other twelve are located across the country. The judges who sit on the Court of Appeals hear appeals from federal district courts located within their areas. People who are dissatisfied with the decision of the district court may take their case to the Court of Appeals that covers their area. The second circuit includes Connecticut, New York, and Vermont.

On June 25, 1997, President Bill Clinton nominated Sotomayor to the vacant seat on the Court of Appeals. She again appeared before the Senate Judiciary Committee, this time at a hearing into her qualifications to become a judge on the Court of Appeals. Senator Moynihan also spoke to the committee. He told them that, as a district judge, Sotomayor "presided over cases of enormous complexity with skill and confidence." He knew she had the experience and the intelligence to sit on the Court of Appeals.

The committee found that Sotomayor was qualified to become an appeals judge. The nomination now had to be voted on by the full Senate. But, before a vote was taken, an article appeared in the *Wall Street Journal*. The article said that Sotomayor's district court rulings showed that she was a liberal activist, someone who supports, and advocates for, the rights of poor and minority people. Conservative radio host Rush Limbaugh saw the article and talked about Sotomayor's being on a "rocket ship" to the Supreme Court. It was rumored that one of the Supreme Court justices might soon retire and that President Clinton, a Democrat, would nominate Sotomayor to fill that seat.

Sotomayor had been an activist while she was in college and in law school. She'd worked hard to increase the number of minority students and teachers there. She'd been on the board of the Puerto Rican Legal Defense and Education Fund, which helped Latinos who felt they'd been discriminated against in matters of housing, jobs, education, and voting rights. She'd also been appointed to the State of New York Mortgage Agency, where she helped poor and minority people who wanted to get a loan in order to buy a home.

But her activism stopped when she became a judge. She resigned from the organizations so there would be no accusations of conflict of

Rush Limbaugh

interest. And there was no evidence of her activism in her rulings as a district court judge. Her rulings showed that she interpreted the law strictly and based her decisions on what she thought the law said. "This is a judge who does not see it as her job to fix all the social ills in the world," said Kevin Russell, a lawyer who analyzed her rulings.

President Clinton's nomination of Sotomayor created conflict with some Republicans. "Basically, we think that putting her on the appeals court puts her in the batter's box to be nominated to the Supreme Court," one senior Republican aide said. "If Clinton nominated her it would put several of our senators in a real difficult position." The Republican senators were afraid that putting Sotomayor on the Supreme Court would make the Supreme Court more liberal in its future rulings than it was currently. In the late 1990s, the majority of Supreme Court judges leaned more toward conservative interpretations of the law.

Senator Patrick J. Leahy, a Vermont Democrat who was a member of the Senate Judiciary Committee saw what the Republicans were doing in another way. "What they are saying is that they have a brilliant judge who also happens to be a woman and Hispanic, and they haven't the guts to stand up and argue publicly against her on the floor [of the Senate]. They just want to hide in their cloakrooms and do her in quietly."

It took the full Senate more than a year to confirm her. Senator Alphonse D'Amato a Republican from New York, eventually helped push through a vote on her confirmation. Sotomayor was finally confirmed in October 1998.

Ninety-six of the one hundred senators voted. Sotomayor was confirmed by a two-to-one margin. "At long last, this day has finally arrived," Senator Leahy said after the votes were counted. Sotomayor took her seat on the appeals court bench on October 18, 1998.

By that time, she had fallen in love again and became engaged to Peter White. At her induction ceremony as an appeals judge, she spoke directly to him. "Peter, you have made me a whole person, filling not just the voids of emptiness that existed before you, but making me a better, a more loving and a more generous person," she said. "Many of my closest friends forget just how emotionally withdrawn I was before I met you."

The engagement didn't last long, though. Sotomayor and White never married.

In 1998, Judge Sotomayor also began teaching at New York University's law school. The following year found her teaching at Columbia University's law school as well. She received honorary law degrees from Herbert H. Lehman College, Princeton University, and Brooklyn Law School.

Sotomayor gave a speech in 2001 at the University of California in Berkeley, California. She spoke about how Supreme Court justices, or judges, make decisions on the cases that come before them. Some of the words she used in that speech would haunt her for years to come. She told her audience, "[Supreme Court] Justice [Sandra Day] O'Connor has often been cited as saying that a wise old man and wise old woman will reach the same conclusion in deciding cases. I am not . . . sure that I agree with the statement . . . I would hope that a wise Latina woman with the richness of her experiences would more often than not reach a better conclusion than a white male who hasn't lived that life."

In that statement, she was referring to the fact that she, as a Latina woman, could understand and relate more to the life that a poor person, including a minority person, has lead than a white man who has lead a life of wealth and privilege. But Republican conservatives jumped on the words. They said that it showed that she could not be an effective and unbiased, or objective, judge.

Her ruling that attracted the most attention was a 2008 case in which she upheld (agreed with the finding of a lower court) an affirmative action program at the New Haven, Connecticut, fire department. Affirmative action refers to policies and laws that were enacted to help eliminate discrimination against people based on race, religion, gender, or national origin.

The New Haven fire department had thrown out the results of a promotion test because only a few minority fire fighters scored well on the test. "It looked like the exam might have been discriminatory against some of the minority test takers. And that was certainly a red flag for the city under the law," said an attorney for the city of New Haven. A group of white fire fighters, who passed the test, sued. They claimed that the city discriminated against them because they were white.

The case was known as *Ricci v. DeStefano*. One of the white fire fighters, who passed the test and was eligible for promotion, was Frank Ricci. The group of white fire fighters sued the city of New Haven in a local trial court and lost. "Every day I go to work, I gotta pin this lieutenant's badge on me, it reminds me I got screwed out of a captain's badge because of the color of my skin," said one white fire fighter. So they took their case to a higher court and appealed the verdict in the Court of Appeals.

Most of the cases heard in the Court of Appeals are heard by a panel of three judges. Judge Sotomayor was one of the three judges who heard *Ricci v. DeStefano*. She asked tough questions of the lawyers who represented both New Haven and the fire fighters. At one point Judge Sotomayor told the lawyer representing the white fire fighters, "We're not asking that unqualified people be hired—the city's not suggesting that. But if your test is going to always put a certain group at the bottom of the pass rate so they're never, ever going to be promoted, and there is a fair test that can be devised, then why shouldn't the city have an opportunity to try to look and see if it can develop that?"

She also told the lawyer representing New Haven, "What they're saying is . . . you shouldn't permit race to be the driving force. You have to look at the test and determine if the test was fair or not. And if you're going to say 'It's unfair,' point to specific ways it wasn't and make sure there really are alternative [sic]."

At the end of the hearing, Sotomayor and the two other judges on the panel agreed with the ruling made by the lower court. They dismissed the

white fire fighters' claim that the city of New Haven had discriminated against them by throwing out the test. "We are not unsympathetic to the plaintiffs' [the white fire fighters'] expression of frustration," but they don't have a "viable" claim under the law.

Jose Cabranes, Sotomayor's mentor at college and afterwards, was also a judge on the Court of Appeals for the Second Circuit. He had been appointed to that court in 1994 by President Clinton. He criticized the finding of the three-judge panel's decision. He said that the judges had handled the Ricci case in a cursory (too quick) way, but that the issue was "indisputably complex and far from well-settled." In his dissenting, or opposing, opinion, Cabranes wrote that the opinion written by the three-judge panel [made] "no reference whatsoever to the constitutional claims at the core of this case." It was the first time Cabranes had disagreed publicly with Sotomayor.

The fire fighters were not satisfied with the panel's ruling. According to the law, they could ask for all thirteen members of the Court of Appeals to issue a ruling. They appealed the ruling to the full court, which, again agreed with New Haven. The fire fighters' lawyers then asked the Supreme Court of the United States to hear the case and it agreed to hear it in a future session.

About this time, rumors began to circulate that Judge Sotomayor was overly aggressive in court and tended to bully many of the lawyers who argued cases before her. "I felt she could be very judgmental in the sense that she doesn't let you finish your argument before she jumps in and starts asking questions," said one lawyer who appeared before Sotomayor in 2008. "She's brilliant and she's qualified, but I just feel that she can be very, how do you say, temperamental."

Judge Guido Calabresi heard the rumors and decided to check them out for himself. Calabresi had been a dean of the Yale Law School when Sotomayor attended the university. He, too, had been appointed in 1994 to the Court of Appeals for the Second Circuit by President Clinton. Now he looked back at all the questions Sotomayor asked the lawyers in the cases she'd heard. He found that the questions she asked and the way she asked them were no different from what other judges did. "So I concluded that all that was going on was that there were some male lawyers who couldn't stand being questioned toughly by a woman. It was sexism in its most obvious form," he said.

Another judge who sat on the appeals court for the second district defended the intensity with which his colleague questioned lawyers who came before her. "Like many of us, she is engaged in the questioning. We regard oral argument as an important opportunity to engage counsel (a lawyer) and probe the issues. She [Sotomayor] does it with skill and balance and she comes to the bench thoroughly prepared," he said.

A third judge agreed with his colleague that the questioning in a court case can sometimes become intense. "And sometimes, judges themselves get involved in the argument. You press a bit, and sometimes some of your colleagues may think you pressed too hard," he said. "But let's be fair. I think there is a difference between tough questioning and demeaning (insulting) questioning, and I haven't seen that line crossed by any of my colleagues."

Sotomayor's friend, Representative Nydia Velazquez of New York, stood up for her friend. She said, "She [Sotomayor] has the responsibility as a judge to question and to challenge. If it's a man, that is 'tough'—it's OK—if it's a woman then somehow she is a bully or has a bad temper." Judge Calabresi agreed with Valazquez. "Some lawyers just don't like to be questioned by a woman. It was sexist, plain and simple," he said in an interview.

Sotomayor herself spoke about how intense and focused she was when she sat on the bench. "When I'm working in particular, I'm extraordinarily focused and people get intimidated by that focus and intensity I bring to the interaction. And it takes people a little bit of time to realize that I'm not forbidding, that I actually am fun-loving, very open and very human," she explained.

She served as a judge on the Court of Appeals for the Second Circuit for eleven years, but that wasn't where her career would end. There was one more promotion still to come, one that would take her to the top of her profession.

Barack Obama, the forty-fourth president of the United States

A SUPREME COURT NOMINATION

I n 2009 Memorial Day fell on Monday, May 25. The holiday found Judge Sotomayor in her New York office waiting for a phone call from the president of the United States. She had been told that President Barack Obama would decide during the holiday weekend who he was nominating for a seat on the Supreme Court of the United States. Associate Justice David Souter had announced his retirement and the president needed to fill the seat. Sotomayor's name was on Obama's list of possible nominees.

She went to her office at eight o'clock that morning to wait for a phone call from the White House. When the call finally came and she spoke to President Obama, her heart began to beat more quickly than normally. She placed her left hand over her chest to slow down the rapid beating of her heart.

Later she told reporters that the president came on the phone and told her that he wanted to announce her as his selection to be the next associate justice of the United States Supreme Court. She said she caught her breath and began to cry. Through her tears she managed to thank the president for nominating her. She also remembered that the

President Obama announces Sonia Sotomayor as his Supreme Court nominee.

president asked her to promise him two things: to remain the person she was and to stay connected to her community. She told him that they were promises she could make and keep because they were things she couldn't change anyway.

The formal announcement of Sotomayor's nomination was scheduled for the following day. She left immediately for Washington, D.C., and the White House, where the announcement would be made. A friend drove the car while she wrote her acceptance speech.

The trip took longer than the usual four hours, she later explained, because a torrential rain started, which knocked out the GPS [Global Positioning System] in the car. Instead of continuing toward Washington, they got lost and headed into Virginia. They pulled over to the side of the road and Judge Sotomayor called a former law clerk. The law clerk got them back on the road toward Washington and they arrived there safely a few hours later than they had expected.

The following day Sotomayor stood next to President Obama in the White House as he announced his nomination. He talked about all the work that goes into the process of selecting a candidate for the Supreme Court and all of the people involved in deciding on that selection. "After completing this exhaustive process," he said, "I have decided to nominate an inspiring woman who I believe will make a great justice:

Judge Sonia Sotomayor of the great state of New York." He said that she was "an inspiring woman" who "faced down barriers" and "overcame the odds" during her lifetime. He was referring to her growing up as a member of a minority group in a poor South Bronx neighborhood.

In her remarks following the president's announcement, Sotomayor said, "My heart today is bursting with gratitude." Then she spoke about how grateful she was for the support of her family, especially her mother, who had brought her to this moment in time. "She worked often two jobs to help support us after dad died," she said about her mother. "I have often said that I am all I am because of her, and I am only half the woman she is." She also mentioned the last time she'd visited the White House. It had been when President Bill Clinton nominated her as a judge in the Court of Appeals. "It was an overwhelming experience for a kid from the South Bronx," she recalled. "Never in my wildest childhood imaginings did I ever envision that moment, let alone did I ever dream that I would live this moment."

When she was nominated to sit on the Court of Appeals, Sotomayor had to go through a confirmation hearing by the Senate Judiciary Committee and then be voted on by the full Senate. Now she would have to be confirmed by both groups again. If confirmed, she would become the first Hispanic Supreme Court justice.

On June 8, a week after the nomination to the Supreme Court, Sotomayor was on her way to the nation's capital again. She had appointments to meet in Washington, D.C., with several of the senators who would be voting to confirm her. She was about to board an airplane at the airport in New York when she stumbled. She fractured (made a small break) in her right ankle. She testified before the Senate Judiciary Committee with her foot in a cast.

Judge Sotomayor submitted some videos of speeches she'd made to the Senate Judiciary Committee as it prepared to investi-

Sonia Sotomayor on the first day of confirmation hearings on July 13, 2009

gate her qualifications for the office of Supreme Court justice. One of the videos was of a speech she had made years earlier. In it, Sotomayor spoke about how affirmative action had benefited her. She said her standardized test scores in high school had not been high enough to have gotten her admitted to Princeton. Affirmative action had helped her get in.

In the video, Sotomayor said, "With my academic achievement in high school, I was accepted rather readily at Princeton and equally as fast at Yale, but my test scores were not comparable to that of my classmates. And that's been shown by statistics, there are reasons for that. There are cultural biases built into testing, and that was one of the motivations for the concept of affirmative action to try to balance out those effects." Conservative Republican senators pointed to that statement as an example of why Judge Sotomayor did not belong on the Supreme Court.

For the most part, the senators on the committee held opinions based on their political party. Democratic senators spoke approvingly of the nomination while Republicans tended to have doubts.

Democratic Senator Chris Dodd of Connecticut said, "President Obama has promised to bring change to Washington and he continues to do that with his choice for Supreme Court Justice. Judge Sotomayor is a highly qualified and historic nominee." Connecticut's other senator, Joseph Lieberman, a Democrat turned Independent, said, "Judge Sotomayor's career represents the best of the American dream, and she possesses distinguished and superior legal credentials."

But Senator Mitch McConnell, a Republican senator from Kentucky, was worried that Sotomayor would not make her decisions based purely on her interpretation

Joe Lieberman

of the law. She would have radical ideas. She would be influenced by her liberal tendencies and by her experiences as a member of a minority group. Because of those worries, he promised that the Republicans would "thoroughly examine her record to ensure she understands that the role of a jurist (judge) in our democracy is to apply the law even-handedly despite their own feeling or personal or political preferences." That was the issue that many Republican senators would talk about during the next few weeks.

When conservative Republican senators accused Sotomayor of being a radical, Robert Morgenthau came to Sotomayor's defense. He wrote an opinion piece in a New York newspaper. In it he said, "To be sure, she is in favor of civil rights, in the sense that she believes there should be fair treatment for all. But that is, of course, the law. And she understands poverty, and does seem willing to accept government action that provides a safety net to the poor. But that is not exactly 'radical'." When they accused her of having benefited from affirmative action laws in order to go to college and law school, Morgenthau was angry. He wrote, "Sotomayor is where she is today because of her talent. Those who insinuate otherwise don't know her, or simply paint her as they do for political reasons having nothing to do with the truth."

The hearings by the Senate Judiciary Committee began in Washington, D.C., on July 13. First, both sides gave their opening statements, which were followed by questions from the senators and answers from Judge Sotomayor.

In her opening statement Judge Sotomayor told the committee, "In the past month, many senators have asked me about my judicial philosophy [how she reaches a decision when she hears a case]. Simple: fidelity to the law. The task of a judge is not to make law—it is to apply the law." She went on to explain, "In each case I have heard I have applied the law to the facts at hand . . . My personal and professional experiences help me listen and understand, with the law always commanding the result in every case."

New York's Democratic senator, Charles Schumer, agreed with Judge Sotomayor. He testified, "I'm not sure how many of this panel can sit here today and seriously suggest that she comes to the bench with a personal agenda," because her decisions in previous cases did not show any bias for or against anyone, but that she applied the law fairly as the law was written.

Patrick Leahy

Robert Morgenthau also testified on the first day of the hearing. He told the senators, "Judge Sotomayor is highly qualified for any position in which a first-rate intellect, common sense, collegiality and good character would be assets . . . President Obama, and for that matter the United States, should be proud to see once more the realization of that central American credo that in this country a hard-working person with talent can rise from humble beginnings to one of the highest positions in the land."

When it was his turn to speak, Senator Patrick Leahy of Vermont spoke about Judge Sotomayor's seventeen years of experience as a judge, first on the district court and then on the Court of Appeals. Senator Leahy was the chairman of the Senate Judiciary Committee. He reminded the senators that Sotomayor would bring "more federal judiciary experience than any nominee to the Supreme Court in nearly 100 years. In truth, we do not have to speculate about what kind of a justice she will be, because we have seen the kind of judge she has been . . . She has been a judge for all Americans and will be a justice for all Americans." Years earlier Leahy had spoken out in favor of Sotomayor's confirmation when she was nominated for a seat on the Court of Appeals.

But the questions of Sotomayor's past activism and her "wise Latina" statement would not go away. Senator Jeff Sessions, a Republican from Alabama, said, "I want to be clear: I will not vote for and no senator should vote for an individual nominated by any president who is not fully committed to fairness and impartiality toward every person who appears before them." And about the "wise Latina" comment that Sotomayor made, he said that people, "assume the nominee misspoke, but the nominee did not misspeak. She is on record as making the statement at least five times over the course of a decade."

When it was her turn to respond, Sotomayor admitted, "I regret that I have offended some people," about the "wise Latina" comments.

Despite the questions some of the conservative Republicans had about Judge Sotomayor's ability to be objective when hearing cases before the Supreme Court, the Democratic senators and most of the Republican senators believed she would be confirmed. Both the Senate Judiciary Committee and the full Senate had more Democratic than Republican senators, and a Democratic president had nominated her. Senator Lindsey Graham, a Republican from South Carolina, told Sotomayor, "Unless you have a complete meltdown, you're going to get confirmed." Graham was one of the Republicans on the committee who was expected to vote to confirm Sotomayor.

Lindsey Graham

On July 28 the hearings were completed and the Senate Judiciary Committee voted. The vote was 13-6 to confirm Sonia Sotomayor for the Supreme Court. Now it would be up to the full Senate.

Many senators spoke to reporters after the vote was taken. They told the reporters why they had voted for or against confirming Sotomayor. Republican Senator Charles Grassley of Iowa voted against her. "Unfortunately, I'm not convinced that Judge Sotomayor will be able to set aside her personal preferences and prejudices," he said.

Senator Graham also spoke to reporters after the vote. As was expected he had voted to recommend her confirmation by the full Senate. He said, "I feel good about Judge Sotomayor. What she will do as a judge I think will be based on what she thinks is right. I haven't seen this activism that we should all dread and reject."

Nevada's Harry Reid, a Democrat who was the Senate Majority Leader, summed up the Democrats' point of view about Judge Sotomayor. He also mentioned his expectations about what would happen when the full Senate voted. He said, "She's developed a 17-year record as a moderate, mainstream judge. I'm disappointed not more of my colleagues on the other side of the aisle (the Republicans) are likely to vote for this outstanding nominee."

Speaking for the Republicans, Senator Mitch McConnell of Kentucky said, "[Sotomayor] is certainly a fine person with an impressive story and a distinguished background. But a judge must be able to check his or her personal or political agenda at the courtroom door and do justice evenhandedly . . . It's a test Judge Sotomayor does not pass."

Before the confirmation vote was taken in the full Senate, Senator Leahy told the senators, "Judge Sotomayor's career and judicial record demonstrates that she has always followed the rule of law. Attempts at distorting that record by suggesting that her ethnicity or heritage will be the driving force in her decisions as a justice of the Supreme Court are

Mitch McConnell

demeaning to women and all communities of color."

The full Senate voted on August 6. They voted 68-31 for confirmation. Only one Senator—Ted Kennedy—did not cast his vote. He was absent from the Senate because he was seriously ill.

People of Latino background were elated that Sotomayor was to be elevated to the highest court in the land. Women's organizations were happy that another woman was to become a Supreme Court Justice. Only two women—Sandra

Day O'Connor and Ruth Bader Ginsburg—had achieved that position before her.

When President Obama learned that his nominee had been confirmed, he said, "These core American ideals—justice, equality, and opportunity—are the very ideals that have made Judge Sotomayor's own uniquely American journey possible. They're ideals she's fought for throughout her career, and the ideals the Senate has upheld today in breaking yet another barrier and moving us yet another step closer to a more perfect union." He praised the Senate for confirming that Sotomayor had the "temperament, the history, the integrity, and the independence of mind to ably serve on our nation's highest court" and he was confident that she "will make an outstanding Supreme Court justice."

Sonia Sotomayor was sworn in as a Supreme Court Justice on August 8.

Supreme Court Justice Sonia Sotomayor

THE JUSTICE TAKES HER SEAT

Sonia Sotomayor was sworn in as an associate justice of the Supreme Court of the United States in two separate ceremonies. Both took place on Saturday, August 8, 2009. One is prescribed or written in the Constitution of the United States and all federal officials are required to take it. The other is spelled out in the Judiciary Act of 1789, which established the federal court system.

The first ceremony was a private one that took place in the Supreme Court. Only Sotomayor's family was present, and the oath was administered by Chief Justice John Roberts.

Sotomayor said, "I, Sonia Sotomayor, do solemnly swear that I will administer justice without respect to persons, and do equal right to the poor and to the rich, and that I will faithfully and impartially discharge and perform all of the duties incumbent upon me as an associate justice of the Supreme Court of the United States under the Constitution and laws of the United States. So help me God." These words are written in the U.S. Constitution and all officials of the federal government, including Supreme Court justices, must take the oath.

The second ceremony, a public one, followed immediately. This time Sotomayor took the oath in front of her family, friends, and the media, including television cameras. The oath was again administered by the chief justice.

Following the swearing-in ceremonies, Sonia Sotomayor became the 111th justice of the U.S. Supreme Court. She also became just the third woman to hold that position, following Sandra Day O'Connor, who had retired in 2006, and Ruth Bader Ginsburg, who still serves.

The Supreme Court was established by Article III of the Constitution of the United States, which states in part, "The judicial power of the United States shall be vested in one Supreme Court, and in such

Members of the U.S. Supreme Court pose for a group photograph at the Supreme Court building on September 29, 2009 in Washington, D.C. Front row, from left to right: Associate Justice Anthony M. Kennedy, Associate Justice John Paul Stevens, Chief Justice John G. Roberts, Associate Justice Antonin Scalia, and Associate

inferior (lower) courts as the Congress may from time to time ordain and establish." Congress passed the Judiciary Act of 1789, which organized the Supreme Court, the federal circuit courts, and the federal district courts. It gave the president the right to nominate justices for the Supreme Court with the approval of the Senate. The justices serve on the court for the rest of their lives or until they decide to retire.

At the time the Supreme Court was organized, it had six justices. One justice was appointed to be chief justice. Congress raised the number of justices to nine, where it remains today.

On August 9, 2009, Sonia Sotomayor joined eight other sitting justices. Five are considered conservatives—John Roberts Jr., Anthony

Justice Clarence Thomas. Back Row, from left to right: Associate Justice Samuel Alito Jr., Associate Justice Ruth Bader Ginsburg, Associate Justice Stephen Breyer, and Associate Justice Sonia Sotomayor

Kennedy, Antonin Scalia, Clarence Thomas, and Samuel Alito Jr.—nominated by conservative presidents. Three are considered liberals—John Paul Stevens, Ruth Bader Ginsburg, and Stephen Breyer—nominated by more liberal presidents. Justices usually reflect the values of the presidents who nominated them. Sotomayor replaced David Souter, a liberal justice, who had retired from the bench.

A Republican president will usually nominate a conservative justice and a Democratic president will usually nominate someone who is more liberal. Justice Sotomayor is expected to be a liberal, based on her rulings during her seventeen years as a judge and the fact that she was nominated by a Democratic president.

President Obama hosted a reception in the East Room of the White House for the new Supreme Court justice on August 12. Robert Morgenthau was one of the invited guests, as were Sotomayor's family and friends, as well as some Hispanic leaders and two of Sotomayor's fellow Supreme Court justices.

With Sotomayor at his side, the president said, "While this [her rise to the Supreme Court] is Justice Sotomayor's achievement, the result of her ability and determination, this moment is not just about her.

The White House

It's about every child who will grow up thinking to him or herself, 'If Sonia Sotomayor can make it, then maybe I can, too.' This is a great day for America." And referring to her seventeen years as a judge, he said, "With her extraordinary breadth and depth of experience, Justice Sotomayor brings to the Court both a mastery of the letter of the law and an understanding of how the law actually unfolds in our daily lives . . ." She had heard both criminal cases and corporate or business cases as a judge in the district court and in the Court of Appeals.

In her response, Sotomayor said, "No words can adequately express what I am feeling. No speech can fully capture my joy in this moment. It is this nation's faith in a more perfect union that allows a Puerto Rican girl from the Bronx to stand here now . . . I am deeply humbled by the sacred responsibility of upholding our laws and safeguarding the rights and freedoms set forth in our Constitution. I ask not just my family and friends, but I ask all Americans, to wish me divine guidance and wisdom in administering my new office."

The Supreme Court is an institution with many traditions. One is that the newest justice sits in the very last seat on the right facing the courtroom. That seat has traditionally been reserved for the newcomer. Another tradition has the newest justice act as a "go-for" when the justices are having private discussions in their conference room. When there is a knock on the door of the conference room, it is the newest justice's job to open the door.

And a third duty to be performed by the newest justice is to keep an accurate vote count when the justices are deciding whether or not to hear a case. If four justices vote to hear a particular case, then that case is added to the docket, which is the list of cases that the Court will hear. The justices have to read through hundreds of cases before deciding on those that they will hear. They usually choose to hear cases that are about important federal issues, those that challenge newly enacted laws passed by Congress and signed by the president, those that change existing federal laws, or those that are about constitutional issues. Most other cases are rejected for consideration.

On September 8 the Supreme Court officially welcomed Justice Sonia Sotomayor to the bench in a special session. The very next day the justices began to hear arguments in an important campaign finance case. They had heard the case in March, during their spring term, or session.

Hillary Clinton

Generally the justices hear cases during two terms, one in the spring and one in the fall. But because of the importance of this case, the Court decided to rehear it during a special summer term. Their decision could influence how future political elections in the United States would be decided.

The case was *Citizens United v. Federal Election Commission*. A conservative advocacy group called Citizens United had made a TV documentary film called *Hillary: The Movie*. The film was critical of Hillary Clinton's character and her career. Citizens United wanted to show the film just before the primary election when everyone thought Clinton would be the democratic candidate for president of the United States in 2008. When the Federal Election Commission refused to allow them to show the film, Citizens United sued. The lower courts ruled against them, so they appealed it all the way to the Supreme Court. At issue was whether the movie is protected by the First Amendment of the Constitution, which guarantees freedom of speech.

In the meantime, Justice Sotomayor had hired four law clerks, the same number that each of the other justices had. Sotomayor told the interviewer that she works in her chambers when she is not actually hearing a case. "I think better in chambers. I also draft on the computer and so I like being at my desk and having everything around me. I also like being able to call out to my law clerks with an idea...or popping out of my desk and running in to them and saying how about this and engaging them with the idea. But I do like working at my desk." The justices' law clerks have their own offices adjacent to their justices' chambers.

When asked about how she writes her opinions, she said, "I welcome the views of my colleagues on every draft that I do and I share with my colleagues my views of ways in which to insure that each issue we're addressing is also—and each draft that we're issuing is addressing the important points that the parties are making and so I guess what they could expect from me is a very interactive colleague both in welcoming their suggestions and incorporating them into drafts and sharing with them my own views as well."

Two weeks after she took her seat on the Supreme Court, Justice Sotomayor was asked by an interviewer about possible mentors she might have among the other justices. She answered that all of the justices have mentored her, or answered her questions. She said, "All of my colleagues have been extraordinarily warm and welcoming. Each one of them has offered advice; each one of them has invited me to call them with questions . . . there's always a question on my mind and when I meet them in the hall I just go up to them and say can you or would you and they've each been delightfully generous in giving me time to walk me through whatever it is that I'm asking about."

Like thousands of men and women, Justice Sotomayor decided that she would have two homes. She needed to keep her condominium apartment in New York. Her reason was very practical. "Right now I— like many other Americans, it would not be wise for me to sell my home in New York because the market is so low," she explained. She also found a place to live in Washington, D.C., so she could get to work easily when the Supreme Court was in session.

On September 26, Justice Sotomayor was back in New York. She was invited by her long-time favorite baseball team, the New York Yankees, to throw out the first ball before the game the Yankees were playing against the Boston Red Sox. "Having Justice Sotomayor, a South Bronx native, participate in our yearly Hispanic Heritage Month celebration is very exciting, as she is an inspiration to so many," said the Yankees' director of Latino affairs. Accompanied by one of the Yankee players and wearing a Yankee shirt, Justice Sotomayor walked to the pitcher's mound to thunderous applause from the fans. She threw the ball to the catcher at home plate and then walked off the field to another round of thunderous applause.

Jorge Posada, number twenty of the New York Yankees, walks Supreme Court Justice Sonia Sotomayor out to the mound during the game on September 26, 2009, at Yankee Stadium in the Bronx borough of New York City.

She returned to Washington, D.C., for the fall term of the Supreme Court, which always begins on the first Monday in October.

On October 5, the first Monday in October 2009, the Supreme Court began its fall term. One of the cases it heard had to do with when questioning may resume after a criminal suspect asks for a lawyer. The case was *Maryland v. Shatzer*.

Michael Shatzer was sent to prison in 2003 for sexual abuse of a child. The police wanted to question him again about another case of child sexual abuse. Shatzer refused to answer, asked for a lawyer, and all questioning stopped.

Every police officer in the United States is required to read or recite the Miranda rights statement to a person who is suspected of having committed a crime. The statement says that the suspect has the right to be represented by a lawyer before being questioned by police. If the suspect cannot afford to hire a lawyer, then one will be provided. The purpose of the Miranda rights statement is to protect a suspect from self-incrimination, or giving information about him or herself that might result in being charged with a crime, or badgering (harassing, pestering, or nagging) by police.

More than two years later, Shatzer spoke to another police officer who was investigating a different case and Shatzer made incriminating comments, which caused him to appear to be guilty, and that got him convicted of a second case of child abuse. His lawyer claimed he should not have been questioned, since he'd asked for a lawyer.

The Maryland attorney general insisted Shatzer should have asked for a lawyer a second time if he wanted one. "He [Shatzer] is not subject to further questioning until a lawyer has been made available or the suspect himself reinitiates conversation," agreed the Maryland Court of Appeals in its decision. It ruled that Shatzer's rights had been violated when he was questioned more than two years later.

The case was appealed to the Supreme Court, which decided it was an important enough case for them to hear. The question for them to decide was how long the prohibition against questioning lasts.

Justice Sotomayor showed the Court that she was not shy about asking questions. When the defense lawyer did not state clearly when a suspect's request to speak with a lawyer before being questioned would end, she asked, "So there is no termination point? Really?" she asked the defense lawyer at one point. She also asked questions about the facts in the case, such as, "Could I have a clarification of the facts for a moment?" and "Are you sure?"

And when a lawyer was too talkative, she asked questions that cut to the essence of the case. In one instance, she asked one of the lawyers, who in this case was Maryland's attorney general, "He [the defendant/suspect] said, 'I don't want to talk to you without a lawyer,' correct?" When he said yes, she asked, "And the state doesn't provide him with a lawyer, correct?" (the case had been argued originally in Maryland) "All right. So what gives him an understanding that one will be provided the next time he's questioned?" That was an important issue in the case.

On October 13 Justice Sotomayor was invited to a White House celebration of Latin music in a tent President Obama and the First Lady had set up on the South Lawn. It was part of the White House Music Series. Each concert in the series focused on a different type of music, and this one was all about Latin music. Many Latino singers and musicians, including Sheila E, Gloria Estefan, Jose Feliciano, Los Lobos, and Mark Anthony performed.

The musicians had their roots in several Latin American countries— Cuba, Mexico, the Dominican Republic, and Puerto Rico. Speaking to the audience, President Obama said, "Even though it's constantly evolving, Latin music speaks to us all in a language we can understand about hope and joy, sorrow and pain, friendship and love. It moves us, and it attempts to make us move a little bit ourselves," he said.

The Supreme Court broke for its Christmas recess. Justice Sotomayor and her mother traveled to Puerto Rico for a visit. Although she had made many visits to her parents' homeland, it was the first time she went as a Supreme Court justice.

Many reporters came to the airport in San Juan, the capital of the island territory, to greet her. At a news conference at the airport, Justice Sotomayor said in Spanish that she and her mother wanted to extend a warm embrace to their beloved island of Puerto Rico. And when reporters asked what she was going to do during her visit, she told them that she and her mother planned to visit family members and to eat *mofongo*, a dish made of mashed plantains.

But she also visited the Museum of Art of Puerto Rico where reporters again questioned her. By this time, her "wise Latina" comment had become famous. There were T-shirts, coffee cups, and buttons with her picture and words being sold on street corners and in gift shops. Sotomayor told the reporters about the number of people who come up to her to hug, kiss, and touch her, some with tears in their eyes. She appreciated that, she said. But then, referring to the items being sold with her picture and her words on them, she said that she wished there was a way of stopping that. She added that she spoke those words without intending that people should make money from them, which seemed wrong to her.

The year 2010 brought a ruling by the Supreme Court in the campaign finance case, which had been argued in October 2009. In a 5-4 decision handed down on January 21, the justices decided that corporations have the same rights as individuals when it comes to political speech and can therefore use their profits to support or oppose individual candidates.

In issuing its ruling, the Supreme Court said that "government may not suppress political speech on the basis of the speaker's corporate identity," meaning that just because the "speaker" was a corporation doesn't mean that it can't make its opinion public. That decision could affect how future political campaigns are waged.

As a Supreme Court justice, Sonia Sotomayor will have a hand in changing people's lives for many years to come. The little girl who at age ten decided to become a judge now sat with eight others at the top of her profession. She had heeded her mother's words about the importance of getting an education. She had studied and worked hard, and she had succeeded beyond her wildest dreams.

TIMELINE

1954   Born on June 25 to Juan and Celina Baez Sotomayor in the Bronx, New York.

1957   Brother, Juan, is born.

1962   Develops juvenile diabetes.

1963   Father dies.

1972   Graduates from Cardinal Spellman High School; enters Princeton University in Princeton, New Jersey; becomes involved with minority organizations at Princeton.

1974   Writes letter to U. S. Department of Health, Education & Welfare urging more minority students and faculty at Princeton.

1976   Wins pretigious M. Taylor Pyne Honor Prize; graduates summa cum laude from Princeton; marries Kevin Noonan in New York during the summer; enters Yale Law School in New Haven, Connecticut in the fall; becomes involved with minority organizations at Yale; becomes editor of Yale Law Journal.

1979   Graduates from Yale Law School; joins the New York district attorney's office as a prosecutor.

1980   Becomes member of board of Puerto Rican Legal Defense and Education Fund.

1983 Divorces Kevin Noonan.

1984 Leaves district Attorney's office; joins law firm Pavia & Harcourt.

1987 Appointed to board of State of New York Mortgage Agency by governor.

1988 Appointed to New York City Campaign Finance Board by mayor; becomes partner at Pavia & Harcourt.

1990 Nominated to be federal judge for Southern District of New York.

1992 Confirmed as a federal judge; resigns from Pavia & Harcourt.

1995 Rules on Vince Foster suicide note; ends baseball strike.

1997 Nominated to Court of Appeals for the Second Circuit.

1998 Confirmed as Court of Appeals judge.

2009 Sworn in as associate justice on Supreme Court on August 8.

SOURCES

CHAPTER ONE:
THE LONG JOURNEY FROM A PUBLIC HOUSING PROJECT

p. 13   "I can only imagine . . ." Lisa Lucus and David Saltonstall, "Sonia Sotomayor's mother tells News: I overcame odds to raise U.S. Supreme Court Pick," *New York Daily News*, May 28, 2009.

p. 14   "There were working poor . . ." Sheryl Gay Stolberg, "Sotomayor, a Trailblazer and a Dreamer," *New York Times*, May 27, 2009.

p. 14   "Being a Latina . . ." Michael Saul, "Obama's Supreme Court pick Sonia Sotomayor never forgot her Bronx roots," *New York Daily News*, May 26, 2009.

p. 15-16   "I became very disappointed . . ." Greg B. Smith, "JUDGE'S JOURNEY TO TOP BRONX' SOTOMAYOR ROSE FROM PROJECTS TO COURT OF APPEALS," *New York Daily News*, October 24, 1998.

p. 16   "I was going . . ." Ibid.

p. 16   "I can remember . . ." Scott Shane and Manny Fernandez, "A Judge's Own Story Highlights Her Mother's," *New York Times*, 28, 2009.

p. 16   "She struggled . . ." Lucas and Saltonstall, "Sonia Sotomayor's mother tells News: I overcame odds to raise U.S. Supreme Court Pick."

p. 17   "On her own . . ." Elaine S. Povich, "Celina Sotomayor: The Nominee's Mother Is 'One Extraordinary Person,'" AARP Bulletin Today, July 14, 2009, http://bulletin.aarp.org/yourworld/family/articles/celina_sotomayor_the_nominee_s_mother_is_one_extraordinary_person_.html.

p. 17   "She knew . . ." Lucas and Saltonstall, "Sonia Sotomayor's mother tells News: I overcame odds to raise U.S. Supreme Court Pick."

p. 17   "My mom was . . ." Shane and Fernandez, "A Judge's Own Story Highlights Her Mother's."

p. 17   "When we left . . ." Robin Shulman, "Supreme Change," *Washington Post*, June 16, 2009.

p. 17   "She worked . . ." Shane and Fernandez, "A Judge's Own Story

Highlights Her Mother's."

p. 18   "She would really listen . . ." Ibid.

p. 18   "a welcoming . . ." Ibid.

p. xx   "Sonia was very much . . ." Stolberg, "Sotomayor, a 18 and a Dreamer."

p. 18   "My Latina identity . . ." Saul, "Obama's Supreme Court pick Sonia Sotomayor never forgot her Bronx roots."

p. 18   "When people . . ." Shane and Fernandez, "A Judge's Own Story

Highlights Her Mother's."

p. 18   "When she would speak . . ." Stephanie Gaskell, "Judge had lots of class," *New York Daily News*, May 31, 2009.

p. 18   "She was smart . . ." Ibid.

p. 19   "I remember . . ." Ibid.

CHAPTER TWO:
A SCHOLARSHIP TO PRINCETON UNIVERSITY

p. 21   "I told her . . ." Stolberg, "Sotomayor, a Trailblazer and a Dreamer," *New York Times*, May 27, 2009.

p. 22   "I felt isolated . . ." James Oliphant, "From Bronx poverty to Ivy League," *Los Angeles Times*, May 27, 2009.

p. 22   "She was intimidated . . ." Evan Thomas, Stuart Taylor Jr., and Brian No, "Meet The Sotomayors," *Newsweek*, July 20, 2009.

p. 22   "very foreign . . ." "Raising the Bar: Pioneers in the Legal Profession," American Bar Association; http://www.abanet.org/publiced/hispanic_s.html.

p. 22   "a visitor landing . . ." Jennifer Ludden and Linton Weeks, "Sotomayor: 'Always Looking Over My Shoulder,'" National Public Radio, May 26, 2009; http://www.npr.org/templates/story/story.php:storyId=104538436.

p. 22   "I found . . ." Stuart Taylor Jr., "Grading Sotomayor's Senior Thesis," *National Journal*, June 2, 2009; http://ninthjustice.nationaljournal.com/2009/06/grading-sotomayors-senior-these.php?

p. 22   "I spent one . . ." Ibid.

p. 23   "She was very studious . . ." Gabriel Debenedetti, "At Princeton, Sotomayor '76 excelled at academics, extracurriculars," *Daily Princetonian*, May 13, 2009; http://www.dailyprincetonian.cm/2009/05/13/23695.

p. 23   "an anchor . . ." "Sonia Sotomayor Biography," http://www.biography.com/articles/Sonia-Sotomayor-453906?.

p. 23   "We were committed . . ." Thomas, Taylor Jr., and No, "Meet The Sotomayors."

p. 24   "The facts imply . . ." Daily Princetonian Staff, "Letter to the Editor: Anti-Latino discrimination at Princeton (May 10, 1974)," *Daily Princetonian*, May 27, 2009; http://www.dailyprincetonian.com/2009/05/27/23731.

p. 24   "The prize . . ." Emily Rutherford, "Sotomayor as a College Activist," *Campus Progress*, July 15, 2009, http://www.campusprogress.org/opinions//4296/sotomayor-as-college-activist?type=.

p. 24   "The kid who . . ." Oliphant, "From Bronx poverty to Ivy League."

p. 25   "the island . . ." Stolberg, "Sotomayor, a Trailblazer and a Dreamer."

p. 25   "My days at Princeton . . ." Thomas, Taylor Jr., and No, "Meet The Sotomayors."

p. 25   "At Princeton . . ." "Peter Winn: Education of Sonia Sotmayor," History News Network, http://hnn.us/roundup/entries/99938.html.

CHAPTER THREE:
ON TO YALE LAW SCHOOL

p. 27   "She seemed to fit . . ." Zeke Miller, "At Yale, Sotomayor was sharp but not outspoken," *Yale Daily News*, May 31, 2009, http://www.yaledailynews.com/news/features/2009/05/31/at-yale-sotomayor-was- sharp-but-not-outspoken/.

p. 27-28   "very personable . . ." Saul, "Obama's Supreme Court pick Sonia Sotmayor never forgot her Bronx roots."

p. 28   "She was always . . ." Richard Lacayo, "Sonia Sotomayor: A Justice Like No Other," *Time*, May 28, 2009.

p. 28   "I remember . . ." Mary E. O'Leary, "High court candidate's ruling scrutinized," *New Haven Register*, May 10, 2009.

p. 28   "career advisor . . ." David D. Kirkpatrick, "Judge's Mentor: Part Guide, Part Foil," *New York Times*, June 22, 2009.

p. 28   "In the near future . . ." Sonia Sotomayor de Noonan, "Statehood and the Equal Footing Doctrine: The Case for Puerto Rican Seabed Rights," *Yale Law Journal* 88, no. 5, (April 1979).

p. 29   "not a topic . . ." Amy Goldstein and Jerry Markon, "Heritage Shapes Judge's Perspective," *Washington Post*, May 27, 2009.

p. 29   "Her work was thorough . . ." Elizabeth Landau, "Sotomayor 'Always Willing to Speak Up' at Yale Law," CNN, May 26, 2009, http://157.166.255.31/2009/POLITICS/05/26/sotomayor.princeton.yale/index.html.

p. 29   "She was . . ." Peter Nicholas and James Oliphant, "Two sides to Sonia Sototmayor," *Los Angeles Times*, May 31, 2009.

p. 29-30   "Do law firms . . ." Stuart Auerbach, "Law Firm Apologizes to Yale Student," *Washington Post*, December 16, 1978.

p. 30   "discriminatory," Ibid.

p. 30   "The firm did not . . ." Ibid.

p. 30   "insensitive . . ." Ibid.

CHAPTER FOUR:
IN THE DISTRICT ATTORNEY'S OFFICE

p. 33   "I asked him . . ." Transcription, "Testimony of District Attorney Robert M. Morgenthau Before the Committee on the Judiciary of the United States Senate," http://www.manhattanda.org/whatsnew/inthenews/2009-07-17.pdf.

p. 34   "I told him . . ." Benjamin Weiser and William K. Rashbaum, "Sotomayor Is Recalled as a Driven Rookie Prosecutor," *New York Times*, June 8, 2009.

p. 34   "to bring . . ." Goldstein and Markon, "Heritage Shapes Judge's Prespective."

p. 34   "She was . . ." Oliphant, "From Bronx poverty to Ivy league."

p. 34   "I just remember . . ." Weiser and Rashbaum, "Sotomayor Is Recalled as a Driven Rookie rosecutor."

p. 35   "My work . . ." Division for Public Education: National Hispanic Heritage Month 2000, American Bar Association, http://www.abenet.org/publiced/

hispanic_s.html.

p. 35   "I had more problems . . ." Stolberg, "Sotomayor, a Trailblazer and a Dreamer," *New York Times*, May 27, 2009.

p. 35   "Once I started . . ." Ibid.

p. 35   "was her patron . . ." Andrew Zajak, "Sotomayor was nudged into judgeship, associates say," *Los Angeles Times*, June 6, 2009.

p. 37   "She had that . . ." Dina Temple-Raston, "Sotomayor's Real-World Schooling In Law And Order," NPR, June 9, 2009, http://www.npr.org/templates/story/story.php?storyId=105005007.

p. 37   "Assistant DA . . ." Transcription, "Testimony of District Attorney Robert M. Morgenthau Before the Committee on the Judiciary of the United States Senate," http://www.manhattanda.org/whatsnew/inthenews/2009-07-17.pdf.

p. 38   "handled it . . ." Greg B. Smith, "JUDGE'S JOURNEY TO TOP BRONX' SOTOMAYOR ROSE FROM PROJECTS TO COURT OF APPEALS," *New York Daily News*, October 24, 1998.

p. 38   "I saw children . . ." "Opening Statement: Judge Sonia Sotomayor," NPR, July 13, 2009, http://www.npr.org/templates/story/story/php?storyId=106551585.

p. 38   "family and friends . . ." Serge F. Kovaleski, "Little Information Given About Solo Law Practice Run by Sotomayor in '80s," *New York Times*, July 7, 2009.

p. 38   "potential superstar," Michael Powell, Serge, F. Kovaleski, and Russ Buettner, "To Get to Sotomayor's Core, Start in New York," *New York Times*, July 10, 2009.

p. 38   "I cannot attribute . . ." Ibid.

CHAPTER FIVE:
ENTERING PRIVATE PRACTICE

p. 41   "I left . . ." "Sotomayor Gives Intimate Look Into
             Personal Life," FOXNews.com, June 12, 2009,
             http://www.foxnews.com/politics/2009/06/12/
             Sotomayor-gives-intimate-look-into-personal-life/

p. 41   "It [her diabetes] . . ." Michael Powell and Serge F.
             Kovaleski, "Sotomayor Rose on Merit Alone, Her
             Allies Say," *New York Times*, June 5, 2009.

p. 41-2   "We had an opening . . ." Stolberg, "Sotomayor, a
             Trailblazer and a Dreamer," *New York Times*, May
             27, 2009.

p. 42   "She was just ideal . . ." Keith B. Richburg, "N.Y.
             Federal Judge Likely on Shortlist," *Washington
             Post*, May 7, 2009.

p. 42   "I focused on . . ." "Opening Statement: Judge Sonia
             Sotomayor," NPR, July 13, 2009, http://www.npr.
             org/templates/story/story.php?storyId=106551585.

p. 42   "As a result . . ." Division for Public Education:
             National Hispanic Heritage Month 2000, American
             Bar Association; http://www.abenet.org/publiced/
             hispanic_s.html.

p. 42   "She had . . ." Doug Gross, "Sotomayor is tough judge
             with breadstick habit, colleagues say," CNN.com,
             http://www.cnn.com/2009/US/07/17/sotomayor.
             bench/index.html#STCText.

p. 43   "required more substantial . . ." Serge F. Kovaleski,
             "Little Information Given About Solo Law Practice
             Run by Sotomayor in '80s."

p. 44   "She floored us," Zajac, "Sotomayor was nudged into
             judgeship, associates say."

p. 44   "She was the youngest . . ." Powell and Kovaleski,
             "Sotomayor rose on Merit Alone, Her Allies Say."

p. 44   "she was very prepared . . ." Zajac, "Sotomayor was nudged into judgeship, associates say."

p. 44   "Ms. Sotomayor . . ." Charlie Savage and Michael Powell, "In New York, Sotomayor Put Focus on the Poor," *New York Times*, June 19, 2009.

p. 45   "I remember . . ." Powell and Kovaleski, "Sotomayor rose on Merit Alone, Her Allies Say."

p. 45   "I had a search . . ." Jason Horowitz, "The Many Rabbis of Sonia Sotomayor," *New York Observer*, May 26, 2009; http://www.observer.com/3719/many- Rabbis-sonia-sotomayor.

p. 45   "While there . . ." CQ Transcriptions, "District Attorney of New York County Robert Morgenthau Testifies at Judge Sotomayor's Confirmation Hearings," *Washington Post*, July 16, 2009.

p. 45   "She was very . . ." Powell and Kovaleski, "Sotomayor rose on Merit Alone, Her Allies Say."

p. 45   "We would be . . ." Ibid.

CHAPTER SIX:
BECOMING A FEDERAL JUDGE

p. 49   "I had always . . ." "Raising the Bar: Pioneers in the Legal Profession," American Bar Association, http://www.abanet.org/publiced/hispanic_s.html.

p. 49   "I just decided . . ." Zajac, "Sotomayor was nudged into judgeship, associates say."

p. 49   "Sonia had . . ." Powell and Kovaleski, "Sotomayor Rose on Merit Alone, Her Allies Say."

p. 49   "His interest . . . " Zajac, "Sotomayor was nudged into judgeship, *associates say.*"

p. 49   "Where did you find her . . ." Horowitz, "The Many Rabbis of Sonia Sotomayor."

p. 50   "The hearing was . . ." Lauren Collins, "NUMBER NINE: Sonia Sotomayor's high-profile debut," *New Yorker*, January 11, 2010.

p. 50   "preclude a private speaker . . ." David L. Hudson Jr., "Sotomayor on the First Amendment," First Amendment Center, May 28, 2009, http://www.firstamendmentcenter.org/analysis.aspx?id=21629.

p. 52   "inmates . . ." Ibid.

p. 52   "the beads are not . . ." Ibid.

p. 53   "I sympathize . . ." Ibid.

p. 54   "You can't grown up . . ." Reynolds Holding, "Sonia Sotomayor: A Look a at Obama's Supreme Court Pick," ABC News, May 26, 2009, http://abcnews.go.com/print?id=7676754.

p. 54   "Some say . . ." Ludden and Weeks, "Sotomayor: 'Always Looking Over My Shoulder.'"

p. 54   "I don't expect . . ." "Judge Sonia Sotomayor bio," WABC, May 27, 2009, http://abclocal.go.com/wabc/story?section-news/politics&id=6831739.

CHAPTER SEVEN:
APPOINTMENT TO THE COURT OF APPEALS

p. 57   "presided over cases . . ." Neil A. Lewis, "After Delay, Senate Approves Judge for Court in New York," *New York Times*, October 3, 1998.

p. 58   "rocket ship," Lauren Collins, "Profiles: NUMBER NINE," *New Yorker*, January 11, 2010.

p. 59   "This is a judge . . ." Nicholas and Oliphant, "Two sides to Sonia Sotomayor."

p. 59   "Basically . . ." Lewis, "G.O.P., Its Eyes on High Court, Blocks a Judge," *New York Times*, June 13, 1998.

p. 59   "What they are saying . . ." Ibid.

p. 59   "At long last . . ." Ibid.

p. 59   "Peter . . ." Powell, Kovaleski, and Buettner, "To Get
             to Sotomayor's Core, Start in New York."

p. 60   "[Supreme Court] Justice . . ." Lacayo, "A Justice Like
             No Other."

p. 60   "I would hope . . ." Jeffrey Rosen, "Where She Really
             Stands on Race," *Time*, June 22, 2009.

p. 60   "It looked like . . ." Jan Crawford Greenburg and
             Ariane de Vogue, "Will Race Discrimination Ruling
             Burn Sonia Sotomayor?," ABC News, May 28,
             2009; http://abcnews.go.com/print?id=76911708.

p. 61   "Every day I go . . ." Ibid.

p. 61   "We're not asking . . ." Nina Totenberg, "Is Sonia
             Sotomayor Mean?," National Public Radio, June
             15, 2009, http://www.npr.org/templates/story/story.
             php?storyId=105343155.

p. 61   "What they're saying is . . ." Ibid.

p. 62   "We are not unsympathetic . . ." Greenburg and de
             62, "Will Race Discrimination Ruling Burn Sonia
             Sotomayor?"

p. 62   "I felt . . ." Jo Becker and Adam Liptak, "Sotomayor's
             Blunt Style Raises Issue of Temperament," *New
             York Times*, May 29, 2009.

p. 62-63   "So I concluded . . ." Nina Totenberg, "Is Sonia
             Sotomayor Mean?"

p. 63   "Like many of us . . ." Larry Neumeister, "Taking the
             measure of Sotomayor's courtroom manner," *San
             Francisco Chronicle*, June 6, 2009.

p. 63   "And sometimes . . ." Becker and Liptak,
             "Sotomayor's Blunt Style Raises
             Issue of Temperament."

p. 63   "She [Sotomayor] . . ." Neumeister, "Taking the
             measure of Sotomayor's courtroom manner."

p. 63   "Some lawyers . . ." Becker and Liptak, "Sotomayor's
             Blunt Style Raises Issue of Temperament."

p. 63   "When I'm working . . ." Neumeister, "Taking the
             measure of Sotomayor's courtroom manner."
p. 63   "indisputably . . ." Rosen, "Where She Really Stands
             on Race."
p. 63   "no reference . . ." Lacayo, "A Justice Like No Other."

CHAPTER EIGHT:
A SUPREME COURT NOMINATION

p. 66-67   "After completing . . ." Transcript, "Remarks by the
             President in Nominating Judge Sonia Sotomayor
             to the United States Supreme Court," May 26,
             2009, http://www.whitehouse.gov/the_press_office/
             Remarks-by- the- President-in-Nominating-Judge-
             Sonia-Sotomayor-to-the-United-States-Supreme-
             Court.
p. 67   "an inspiring woman," Zeke Miller, "Sotomayor LAW
             '79 nominated to Court," *Yale Daily News*, May
             26, 2009, http://www.yaledailynews.com/news/
             university- news/2009/05/26/sotomayor-law-79-
             nominated-to-court/.
p. 67   "My heart . . ." Ibid.
p. 67   "She worked often . . ." Ana Radelat, "Obama
             Chooses First Hispanic to Supreme Court,"
             AARP, http://www.aarp.org/content/aarp/en/
             home/makeadifference/advocacy/articles/
             obama_chooses_first hispanic_to_supreme_court.
             html?CMP=KNC-3601.
p. 67   "It was an overwhelming experience . . ." Peter
             Baker and Jeff Zeleny, "Obama Hails Judge as
             'Inspiring,'" *New York Times*, May 27, 2009.
p. 68   "With my academic achievement . . ." Charlie
             Savage, "Videos Shed New Light on Sotomayor's
             Positions," New York Times, June 11, 2009.

p. 68	"President Obama . . ." Miller, "Sotomayor LAW '79 nominated to Court."
p. 69	"Judge Sotomayor's career . . ." Ibid.
p. 69	"thoroughly examine . . ." Ibid.
p. 9	"To be sure . . ." Robert Morgenthau, "Those labeling Sonia Sotomayor a radical don't know her at all," New York Daily News, May 27, 2009.
p. 69	"Sotomayor is . . ." Ibid.
p. 69	"In the past month . . ." Jeffrey Toobin, "Comment: Answers to Questions," *New Yorker*, July 27, 2009, http://www.newyorker.com/talk/comment/2009/07/27/090727taco_talk_toobin.
p. 9	"In each case..." Ari Shapiro, "Sotomayor: 'Fidelity To The Law Guides Me," National Public Radio, July 13, 2009, http://www.npr.org/templates/story/story.php?storyId=1064929000.
p. 69	"I'm not sure..." "Sotomayor pledges 'fidelity to the law,'" CNN.com, July 17, 2009, http://cnn.com/2009/POLITICS/07/13/sotormayor.hearing/index.html.
p. 70	"Judge Sotomayor . . ." CQ Transcriptions, "District attorney of New York County Robert Morgenthau Testifies at Judge Sotomayor's Confirmation Hearings, Washington Post, July 16, 2009.
p. 70	"more federal judiciary . . ." Shapiro, "Sotomayor: 'Fidelity To The Law' Guides Me."
p. 70	"I want to be clear . . ." "Sotomayor pledges 'fidelity to the law'."
p. 70	"assume the nominee . . ." Ibid.
p. 71	"I regret . . ." David Stout, "Senate Likely to Vote on Sotomayor by Early August," New York Times, July 17, 2009.
p. 71	"Unless you have . . ." "Sotomayor pledges 'fidelity to the law'."

p. 71   "Unfortunately . . ." David G. Savage and Mark
               Silva, "Sonia Sotomayor wins backing of Senate
               committee," *Los Angeles Times*, July 28, 2009.
p. 72   "I feel good . . ." Ibid.
p. 72   "She's developed . . ." Julie Hirschfeld Davis,
               "Senate to start historic debate on Sotomayor, in
               line to become Supreme Court's first Hispanic,"
               Chicago Tribune, August 4, 2009, http://www.
               chicagotribune.come/news/politics/sns-a--us-
               sotomayor-senate, 0,4677731.story.
p. 72   "[Sotomayor] is . . ." Ibid.
p. 72   "Judge Sotomayor's . . ." James Oliphant and David
               G. Savage, "Senate confirms Sonia Sotomayor for
               Supreme Court," *Los Angeles Times*, August 6,
               2009.
p. 73   "Those core American ideals . . ." Joseph Williams,
               "Sotomayor confirmation breaks barrier,"*Boston
               Globe*, August 7, 2009.
p. 73   "temperament . . ." Ibid.

CHAPTER NINE:
THE JUSTICE TAKES HER SEAT

p. 78-79   "While this . . ." Jennifer Loven, "Obama, Sotomayor
               celebrate," *Chicago Tribune*, August 13, 2009,
               http://www.chicagotribune.com/news/chi-tc-nw-
               sotomayor-0812- 0813aug13,0,6537496.story.
p. 79   "With her extraordinary . . ." Tony Mauro, "A
               White House Celebration for Sotomayor,"
               Law.com, August 13, 2009, http://law.com/
               LawArticleFriendly.jsp?id=1202432993751.
p. 79   "No words . . ." Ibid.

p. 80	"I think better . . ." Transcript of September 16, 2009 C-SPAN interview by Susan Swain; broadcast October 2009 on C-SPAN program called *Justices Sotomayor, Breyer, & Thomas Interviews,* http://supremecourtc-span.org/assets/pdf/SSotomayor.pdf.
p. 81	"I welcome . . ." Ibid.
p. 81	"All of my colleagues . . ." Ibid.
p. 81	"Right now . . ." James Gordon Meek, "Sonia Sotomayor not selling Greenwich Village pad over weak housing market," *New York Daily News,* October 3, 2009.
p. 81	"Having Justice Sotomayor . . ." Marc Carig, "Supreme Court justice Sonia Sotomayor to throw out first pitch at NY Yankees game," September 22, 2009, http://www.nj.com/yankees/index.ssf/2009/09/supreme_court_justice_sonia_so.htm.
p. 83	"He [Shatzer] is not subject . . ." Robert Barnes, "Sotomayor Takes Active Role on Court's First Day," *Washington Post,* October 6, 2009.
p. 83-84	"So there is no . . ." David G. Savage, "New Justice Sotomayor Asks a Lot of Questions," *Chicago Tribune,* October 6, 2009, http://www.chicagotribune.com/topic/sns-dc-court-otomayor-,9,1354567/story.
p. 84	"Could I have . . ." Adam Liptak, "Sotomayor Puts Stamp on a Day in Court," *The New York Times,* October 10, 2009.
p. 84	"He said . . ." Ibid.
p. 85	"government may not . . ." Roger Parloff, "Behind the Supreme Court ruling in the Citizens United cases," *Fortune,* February 12, 2010.

BIBLIOGRAPHY

Axtell, James. *The Making of Princeton University*. Princeton, New Jersey: Princeton University Press, 2006.

Baum, Lawrence. *The Supreme Court* (8th Edition). Washington, D.C.: CQ Press/Congressional Quarterly Inc., 2004.

Calabrese, Marianne Pilgrim, and Susanne Mary Calabrese. *So You Want to Be a Lawyer?* Hollywood, Florida: Frederick Fell Publishers, Inc., 2005.

Cross, Frank B. *Decision Making in the Court of Appeals*. Stanford, California: Stanford University Press, 2007.

Irons, Peter. *A People's History of the Supreme Court*. New York: Penguin Books, 1999, 2006.

Jenkins, Stephen. *The Story of the Bronx*. Bowie, Maryland: Heritage Books, Inc., 2003.

Kroger, John. *Convictions: A Prosecutor's Battles Against Mafia Killers, Drug Kingpins, and Enron Thieves*. New York: Farrar, Straus and Giroux, 2008.

Mayer, Martin. *The Judges*. New York: Truman Talley Books/St. Martin's Press, 2006.

Nieto, Sonia, ed. *Puerto Rican Students in U.S. Schools*. Mahwah, New Jersey: Lawrence Erlbaum Associates, Publishers, 2000.

Peppers, Todd C. *Courtiers of the Marble Palace: The Rise and Influence of the Supreme Court Law Clerk*. Stanford, California: Stanford University Press, 2006.

Posner, Richard A. *How Judges Think*. Cambridge, Massachusetts: Harvard University Press, 2008

Samtur, Stephen M., and Martin A. Jackson. *The Bronx Then & Now.* Scarsdale, New York: Back in THE BRONX Publishing, 2008.

Segal, Jeffrey A., Harold J. Spaeth, and Sara C. Benesh. *The Supreme Court in the American Legal System.* New York: Cambridge University Press, 2005.

Sheldon, Charles H., and Linda S. Maule. *Choosing Justice: The Recruitment of State and Federal Judges.*

Pullman, Washington: Washington State University Press, 1997. Smith, Richard D. *Princeton University.* Charleston, South Carolina: Arcadia Publishing, 2005.

Sunstein, Cass R., David Schkade, Lisa M. Ellman, and Andres Sawicki. *Are Judges Political? An Empirical Analysis of the Federal Judiciary.* Washington, D.C.: Brookings Institution Press, 2006.

Toobin, Jeffrey. *The Nine: Inside the Secret World of the Supreme Court.* New York: Doubleday, 2007.

WEB SITES

HTTP://WWW.NYC.GOV
> The official Web site of New York City.

HTTP://WWW.NYSD.USCOURTS.GOV/
> The official Web site of the United States District Court for the Southern District of New York.

HTTP://WWW.CA2.USCOURTS.GOV/
> The official Web site of the Court of Appeals for the Second Circuit.

HTTP://WWW.SUPREMECOURT.GOV/
> The official Web site of the Supreme Court of the United States.

INDEX

CREDITS

48	Courtesy of the U.S. Government
51	Used under license from iStockphoto.com
52	Courtesy of the United States Government
53	Used under license from iStockphoto.com
55	Courtesy of the United States Government
56	Alex Wong/Getty Images
58	William Thomas Cain/Getty Images
61	Used under license from iStockphoto.com
64	Courtesy of the United States Government
66	Chip Somodevilla/Getty Images
67	Courtesy of the U.S. Government
68	Courtesy of the U.S. Government
70	Courtesy of the U.S. Government
71	Courtesy of the U.S. Government
72	Courtesy of the U.S. Government
74	Courtesy of the U.S. Supreme Court
76-77	Mark Wilson/Getty Images
78	Courtesy of UpstateNYer
80	Courtesy of the U.S. Government
82	Jared Wickerham/Getty Images